Extending the Invitation

Extending *the* Invitation

*Participating in God's gracious call
to Muslims*

John A. Forrester

Pastor's Attic Press. com

Toronto

In memory of

Necati, Uğur, and Tilmann

who gave their lives for Jesus

April 18th, 2007

Contents

Extending the Invitation

A few years ago, on the lookout for new ideas and fresh perspectives, I wandered over to the beautiful new St. Patrick's Roman Catholic Church building on Main Street in Vancouver, British Columbia. There, carved in stone over the wide oak entrance doors, are these words: "Welcome, The Banquet is Prepared!" I was deeply moved. What a warm greeting. It captures the gracious hospitality of God and his open heart towards us. It reminds me of one of my favorite sayings of Jesus:

And people will come from east and west,
  and from north and south,
  and recline at table in the kingdom of God (Luke 13:29).

What a wonderful picture of rest, reconciliation, redeemed community, and confident celebration.

We Christians love to eat together. In our Baptist church we often joke about spending more time in the kitchen than the sanctuary. But in the world of the Middle East eating together takes on even more significance. Eating together is a sign of belonging. When you are invited to the table you are no longer a stranger, an outsider, you are one of us—you are family.

This is why the religious leaders were so scandalized when Jesus ate with "sinners and tax collectors." This wasn't just a meal. By eating with them he was identifying himself with them, saying, "These are my people." There is no greater privilege than to be invited to the table in the household of God. Once we were all aliens, transients, orphans. Now we have a place, a home, and a new identity—a seat at the table.

This is a book about sharing our Christian faith. It is about inviting others to the banquet. My wife Betty and I spent almost three years in Turkey. So the thoughts and meditations here are shaped by that experience. How do we extend the invitation into a different culture? In particular, how do we extend the invitation to Muslims?

But what we learned in a distant country is just as important to us back in Canada. In our own apartment building we share space with people from around the world, including many from the Middle East. We walk only a few steps to visit our friends in the next apartment, but we cross into a cultural environment that is a world apart from our own. Cross-cultural ministry is no longer a specialty for distant workers, it is part of everyday life in Western cities of the 21st century.

Our neighbours may look and sound very strange to us. And, in fact, they do see the world very differently. Yet how much they are loved by their Father in Heaven, who knows all their unpronounceable names! When our neighbours are no longer strangers to us we will no longer be afraid of them. We will love them too—and remember their names! Will we have the courage to accept their hospitality? As we grow closer we will find that our deepening relationship is itself an invitation to the heavenly banquet.

Although Turkey is often considered to be part of Europe (check, for example, the BBC web site!) the culture is largely that of the Middle East. There might be a veneer of Western ways, but scratch the surface and you encounter values and customs with roots in another world. So we know first hand the legendary hospitality of the Middle East. We have enjoyed many meals in Muslim homes and drunk countless glasses of tea. And because of this the New Testament image of the banquet has come alive for us in a new way. It is a powerful expression of the Gospel.

I have called this little study *Extending the Invitation* because it builds on the image of the banquet. We who follow Christ have eaten at God's table and it has been very good. Now we invite others to come and share in God's extraordinary hospitality.

The word *extending* also suggests the outward movement of the Gospel. It is one thing to extend the invitation to family and friends. It is another to cross the street to a stranger, or to reach out to a new immigrant. But the invitation must go out. Jesus said the invitation would be extended from Jerusalem, to Judea, to Samaria, and to the ends of the earth.

Is he being realistic?—Absolutely! God is well able to finish what he starts. In fact we already have a snapshot of the great outcome:

After this I looked, and behold, a great multitude that no one could number, from every nation, from all tribes and peoples and languages, standing before the throne and before the Lamb... (Revelation 7:9).

The question for us now is how do we get there from here? What is our part in this great drama? Of course there is no single answer to these questions. But what we do know is that God is calling us to participate in his ministry of grace in this world.

The truth is, once we have tasted the banquet, we long to invite others. It is an invitation that comes from the heart. In the pages that follow I will share stories and make observations on extending the invitation, particularly to Muslims and other people from the Middle East. Most of the names are changed, but the events are real. The Scripture quotations are from the English Standard Version.

1. Be Still and Know

We were nearing the end of our time in Istanbul and preparing to move east and south to Adana (next door to Paul's Tarsus). We had enjoyed living in the little district of Küçükyalı with its village-like atmosphere away from the more Westernized center of this immense city of seventeen million people. We had especially enjoyed getting to know our neighbours. Almost certainly we were the first Christians to live in that apartment building, but we had been warmly welcomed. Then, as we talked about our experience there, Betty said,

"It is not by accident that we are in this building with these neighbours. I feel that God has prepared this from the beginning of time. I want to make the most of this opportunity." And off she went for one more visit with Nimet next door. It was a good reminder to me that God is at the center.

For God truly is at the center. And we must emphasize this reality from the beginning. How we need a renewed sense of the sovereignty of God and his overarching plans. Mission is not about us, it is about God. Mission starts with God. Psalm 46:10 calls us back to basics.

Be still, and know that I am God.
I will be exalted among the nations,
I will be exalted in the earth!

What confidence, what hope, what expectation this gives us! God is on his throne. All of the past is in his left hand, all of the future is in his right hand. One day he will bring to completion everything according to his will. God is fulfilling his plans according to his schedule. No part of this planet, no mountain village, no down-town office falls outside the blueprint. God is God. We begin by ceasing from our own activity to become attentive first to God himself.

From duty to delight

What does the sovereignty of God mean to us? For one thing it lifts the weight of responsibility for mission off our shoulders. Mission does not begin or end with us. Yes, God calls us and sends us out. But is this because he can't get the job done without us?—hardly! Surely it would be much easier for him to do this himself. So why does he send us out?

Some people attempted to commiserate with what they thought was the hardship of our time overseas. We spilled the wind out of their sails by telling them how much fun we had! We think of the dear friends, both Muslim and Christian, we would never have known if we had not gone. We will never know in this world all the reasons God directs our paths as he does, but we have discovered one reason to be active in mission—for the joy of it! It is a tremendous privilege.

Paralysis?

But perhaps this reminder of the sovereignty of God is paralyzing. Perhaps we are afraid to make a move because we might step outside the "will of God," or worse, derail God's plan in some area. We need to get over this! Is it really possible that our initiative will undermine the sovereignty of God? What kind of sovereignty would that be?

To know this God of Heaven and Earth is to be freed, not frozen. Yes, we will make mistakes. With all our prayers and the best of advice and a healthy knowledge of God's Word, we will still make mistakes. But even our mistakes are caught up in the plans of God—he saw them coming and adjusted accordingly. We have a shepherd who loves his sheep and knows how to lead them. Even the one who stubbornly insists on heading down the wrong trail will not be abandoned.

No, the doctrine of the sovereignty of God is not paralyzing. When we connect the sovereignty of God with the love of God we discover we can take up our bed and walk, and walk and walk... all the way to Istanbul if we want to, or even to the strange new neighbours across the hall!

He is there first

Behold,
I send an angel before you to guard you on the way
and to bring you to the place
that I have prepared (Exodus 23:20).

Mission begins with God. This means that wherever we go we discover that He is there first. We find that Jesus goes ahead to prepare a place for us, not only in the life to come but also in this life. This is partly for our personal encouragement and benefit, like the furnished apartment he prepared for us in Küçükyalı, and Alev, our wonderful landlady. Partly this is about the privilege of being included in what God is doing in someone else's life.

For two years we prayed about how to get a Bible into the hands of Rıfat. He is the husband of Betty's good friend Songül, both devout Muslims. Before we left to return to Canada we exchanged some gifts. Last of all, respecting his place as head of the family, I gave Rıfat a Turkish Bible. When he saw what it was he suddenly got up and left the room. Oops!... Had I pushed the envelope too far? Then, after a few minutes, he returned. In his hand was a New Testament. I asked him where he got it. He said he bought it from an *eskici*, a street guy who buys and sells old stuff. Rıfat loves books and when he saw this strange but nicely bound volume on the *eskici's* hand cart he just couldn't let it slip by. So he redeemed it for one lira. He took it home and read it and kept it.

God was at work in Rıfat's life long before we met him. Does this mean our time there was wasted? No, it means that God has graciously included *us* in His plans for this man's life. God has added to that earlier work our presence. Now, not only does Rıfat have the written Word of Scripture to account for in his understanding of life, he also has two living Christians to account for, people that he has come to love and respect. We think God is closing in on this family and we pray for them often.

The fingerprints of God
A famous actress said that when she sees food looking that good on the plate she just knows that someone's fingers have been all over it! It's a thought guaranteed to dampen our appetites... unless we love the person who owns the fingers.

Sometimes the fingerprints of God are almost too obvious! While we were in Adana our international congregation held a baptism service in the Mediterranean sea. One woman, who had spent long months preparing for baptism, was unable to go because of family troubles. Then, thankfully, a couple of weeks later she was able to attend a small early morning ceremony at a nearby lake. As she was preparing to go into the water a shepherd, leading a few sheep, and carrying a lamb in his arms, wandered right through the group of people gathered. Only the Lord could choreograph that! "Rejoice with me, for I have found my sheep that was lost," Luke 15:6.

Generally the fingerprints of God are more subtle. We are simply provided for in unexpected ways—including sizable financial gifts to our ministry from people we hardly know. Or a concern is unexpectedly answered. For example one of our dilemmas before we left for Turkey was what to do with our faithful dog Caleb. Then, just in time, we got a call from the administrator of a senior's residence. She wanted Caleb to complement their team of pets who give companionship to the residents. After successfully surviving his job interview (the professional shampoo surely helped), not only did he have a good home, he had an important ministry too!

I suspect that most of the time the fingerprints have been modestly wiped clean. We have no idea of the amount of loving arrangement that goes on for our benefit. But when we are attentive, suspicion mounts. We enjoy the sense of being cared for. We anticipate the unexpected. Creation itself seems transformed. It is the work of a friend, not a stranger. Behind every tree God lurks, plotting good. This is the invigorating context of mission.

Stewards of the honour of God

Why mission? Yes, we do mission because people have needs. The Christian Gospel wonderfully addresses both the here-and-now needs as well as the hereafter needs of this world's troubled people. But if our mission is driven primarily by human need it will not hold, it will run out of steam. Conversely when our mission is God-centered it will go from strength to strength. Here are the familiar opening words of Psalm 100.

> *Make a joyful noise to the Lord, all the earth!*
> *Serve the Lord with gladness!*
> *Come into his presence with singing!*
> *Know that the Lord, he is God!*
> *It is he who made us, and we are his;*
> *we are his people, and the sheep of his pasture.*

What is this? It is a call to worship, worship that arises out of an understanding of who God is and who we are in relation to him. But it is also a call to mission. This *whole* earth should be dancing with joy before the Lord.

Do you remember that old evening hymn: *The day thou gavest Lord, is ended?* It pictures the earth "rolling onwards," "each continent and island" in turn taking up the praises of God—a wave of worship following the daylight around the planet. While we were sleeping last night my dear brother Can, in southeast Turkey, was repairing shoes. Through the long hard hours, as his hands worked, his heart worshiped. He meditated on the text he will use for this Sunday's sermon. As he chatted with customers he bravely steered the conversation towards Christ. Then he slept and now it is our turn to worship. After us China will awake once again. Round and round the planet, God being named, God being worshipped, God being honoured for who he is… Why?—because there is no God like him. He is the great "I am."

But there are still dead spots on this planet. There are still places where God is not honoured as he should be. There are still whole countries where the light of true worship barely flickers. There are still languages that are not used to glorify God. There are still neighbourhoods with no churches to sing his praises. There are still homes where God's name is only used to curse.

Why is mission necessary? Mission is firstly about God's honour. God has put his honour into our hands. He has made us stewards of his honour. He has put his reputation into our care for safe-keeping.

After living for a few years in the honour-shame culture of the Middle East we have a better understanding of this biblical concern for the honour and glory of God. We are more sensitive to our own honour. We realize too that we are confronted with the awesome alternative of either building God's honour or burying it.

Mission magnifies the honour of God. Mission will be complete when God is worshiped and honoured as he should be. Why is mission necessary? Mission is necessary because the worship of God is incomplete.

So when we think about extending the invitation we begin at the beginning. We begin with God. We quiet our scheming hearts before the King of kings. We are still in his holy presence. It is not true that to be so heavenly minded is to be no earthly good. The more we are attentive and present to God, the more we will be attentive and present to people.

....

O Lord, do you not care about your honour?
Have you forgotten your name?

Glorify yourself in this country and that country.
Break in on our comfortable neighbourhoods.
Raise up people who will magnify your name not minimize it.

Wake up O Lord, because the day is slipping away.

And begin with my own attention-deficient heart.
Teach me to be still in your presence.

I pray in the name of the One
who lived only to bring glory to his Father,
Amen.

2. Hey. . . Nice Feet!

But how are they to call on him
in whom they have not believed?
And how are they to believe in him
of whom they have never heard?
And how are they to hear without someone preaching?
And how are they to preach unless they are sent?
As it is written,
"How beautiful are the feet of those
who preach the good news!" Romans 10:14-15

We were all set to leave for Turkey. Our tickets were bought. Our few remaining belongings were packed for travel. We had said more goodbyes than we thought possible. Our financial support was in place. People were praying for us. Then, with just ten days to go, I injured my foot. I carelessly stuck it in front of a boat propeller. The blood flowed thick and red. There was a long anxious moment as I tried to assess the extent of the damage. Thank you Lord! It was only skin deep. Just the scar remains today, but it looked messy for a while with a dozen stitches patching up the damage. As we got on the plane someone quipped, "How beautiful is the *foot* of him who brings the good news!"

Mission work is foot work. We can't escape that. We can't extend the invitation without, in some sense, going out. The Great Commission begins with the verb "go." If there is no going there is no mission. Behind my own carelessness in the water that day was Satan also active? Was he prompting injury at the critical place—the feet? Was this an attempt to sabotage the venture where it really counts?

Confessing inertia

You see the car stalled in the intersection. You run to help get it rolling, leaning at a steep angle and pushing hard. But once it does start moving everyone straightens up and eases off. A light push is all it takes to keep it moving. The inertia has been overcome.

In order to extend the invitation we have to overcome a kind of spiritual inertia. It is hard to get going. It is hard to get out. It is hard because going means leaving. It means leaving the familiar. It means leaving our comfort zone. The old place may not even be a comfortable place, but at least it is a known place. Better the devil you know than the devil you don't!

It is also hard because going means entering a new space. It is a space we cannot fully know until we have actually arrived. It is a space we can only partially anticipate, and we don't like surprises. There are no guarantees. When we go we lose control. But we cannot extend the invitation without, in some sense, going.

This inertia problem is one reason why it is so important to begin with God. As the reality of God and his sovereignty settles in our bones, going out is less threatening. Because David's song has become our song:

Where shall I go from your Spirit?
Or where shall I flee from your presence?
If I ascend to heaven, you are there!
If I make my bed in Sheol, you are there!
If I take the wings of the morning
and dwell in the uttermost parts of the sea,
even there your hand shall lead me,
and your right hand shall hold me (Psalm 139:7-10).

Let's name it for what it is. The inertia problem is really a faith problem. Lord, help me in my unbelief. Lord, help us corporately in our unbelief. Forgive me Lord for not trusting you. Here, inside my circle, I can limit liability, I can manage risk. Out there only God knows.... Forgive me Lord, for trusting more in myself than in you.

Chased out
It was a sickening feeling. The stark white letters on the black screen in front of me announced a serious system failure. The hard drive had crashed on our laptop. Why Lord? I know it's only a computer, but we don't have much left of this world's goods. We let go of almost everything when we came to Turkey. Does this have to go too? Besides, if you had warned me I would have backed up some items....

But it got me out of the house. It got me out of my new little zone of comfort that I was already establishing after just a few months in that new land. That's why I walked into the little computer store in our neighbourhood. A cold call—not knowing anyone, not knowing what to expect, not even knowing the language—simply needing help. And I got help.

The sharp young technician named Armağan (meaning "gift"!) managed to salvage almost all the data off the hard drive. Then he partitioned off the damaged sector and got me up and running again. All for a tenth of what that would have cost in Canada.

But that's not all. In the process I met Serkan, the guy at the front desk. Serkan is an engineering student now preparing to do masters studies in English. We started meeting a couple of times a week trading "English time" for "Turkish time." What a great opportunity to extend the invitation. One week we went over Psalm 23 together. We read it through a number of times both in Turkish and in English and he checked my work on the grammar and vocabulary. He seemed interested and I gave him a copy in both languages to take home. Please Lord, lead him into a Psalm 23 relationship with yourself.

Most English translations begin the Great Commission with the command, "Go!" But technically what is being translated there is not an imperative, but a participle, just as "baptizing" and "teaching" are also participles. A strictly literal translation of the Great Commission would begin: "Going, make disciples...." In more readable form this would be: "As you go, make disciples..." or: "While you go, make disciples...."

My point is this. I'm not arguing that the translations are wrong. Participles sometimes carry the force of a command. But strictly speaking Jesus wasn't commanding us to go out. Why?—because he knew we wouldn't obey! He was simply saying to the disciples, "You *will* go out. I'll make *sure* you go out. And as you go, this is what you are to do." In other words putting this closer to the indicative, rather than the imperative, gave it the weight of prophecy. This is what *will* happen. God in his sovereign love will see to it. Our hesitant human activity is underwritten by the confident activity of God. Again we are alerted to the priority of God in mission.

Is it true that we are slow to obey the command to get out? We only have to look at the book of Acts to find confirmation. Jesus laid out the blueprint: "and you will be my witnesses in Jerusalem and in all Judea and Samaria, and to the end of the earth" (also a prophecy rather than a command!) Did the believers stumble over each other signing up for cross-cultural ministry? No. It was hard to leave Jerusalem. Acts 8 tells us that it took a "great persecution" to get them out of town. Until at last, "Those who were scattered went about preaching the Word."

How wonderful when we can choose to go out. And not just at age twenty, but at forty and sixty and eighty. We have dear friends in Adana who have devoted their retirement years to serving the little international church there. But if we don't choose to go, we should not be surprised if we find ourselves going anyway. If God loved this world enough to send his only son out of the house he won't lose sleep over sending us out of the house. God has his ways. A crashed hard drive?... Well, it meant the invitation got extended to Serkan.

On the road together

Betty and I got to join a group of pastors on a tour of historic Christian sites in Turkey. What fun we had!—getting to know each other, swapping stories at the back of the bus, singing together, picking up new jokes.... We prayed together too, and read Scripture. We also wept together as we discovered one had a serious illness. At each stop a different member of the team would preach through a text relating to that site. At one place we were almost drowned out by the sermon thundering from the loudspeakers of the nearby mosque. There was a keen sense of competition. As we were blessed by our preaching, others looked over our shoulders. One woman watched and listened intently from her third floor balcony. The missional element of our worship was strong.

I am uncomfortable with the phrase, "the missional church." I don't believe the church is primarily about mission as that phrase might suggest. When mission becomes the central focus of the church, the church is no longer church but parachurch. We need parachurch, but we also need church. The church is primarily about worship. Everything else flows out from that. Nevertheless, a church that is not missional is a sick church. How can we experience authentic worship and not want to share it?

As I meditate on the Great Commission I am sometimes overwhelmed by the weight of it. It's a lot to ask! But there is encouragement. I have discovered that this is a *corporate* commissioning. That central imperative, "make disciples," is in the second person *plural*. It is the disciples *as a group* that are being commissioned. And through them, to us as a church. We are called, *together*, to fulfill the Great Commission.

As we move on from the intense individualism of the 20th century into a greater appreciation of community, the call to extend the invitation comes alive with new possibilities. I predict for the 21st century less emphasis on training "soul-winners" and more emphasis on nurturing evangelistic congregations. As each individual contributes his or her unique gifts and abilities the whole church begins to bubble with contagious joy. Often now when we ask new converts who led them to the Lord they list multiple contacts. Corporate evangelism is richer and healthier.

So the question is not just, "How do *I* get out?" but, "How do *we* get out?" How does the church, as a community, extend the invitation? We meet in buildings that are fixed in time and space. We inhabit a particular place with unique GPS coordinates. Though we might be congregational in theory, we are, in fact, parish-dwellers. The kind of church-on-a-bus experience Betty and I enjoyed is possible occasionally, but it can never be normal. We are earthed, we have a home, and rightly so. How then can we be a missional community?

The breathing analogy helps. Sunday morning is like breathing in. We re-group, re-orient, re-fresh. Then we breath out, we split, we disperse. Just as the body can't survive on only in-breaths or only out-breaths, the healthy church, too, cycles in and out, gathering and dispersing. But let's be realistic. It is easier to be intentional about gathering. Can we be more intentional about dispersing missionally?

Healthy churches remember that grace is portable! One believer is a great baker. She takes a blueberry pie to the new neighbour. "Here is my phone number. If you need anything give me a call." Another helps repair a lawnmower. Someone else has a gift for sharing her testimony in a compelling way. One man is intentional about running his business for the glory of God—and it shows. Is it any wonder that outsiders get caught up in the incoming tide as the church gathers again next

Sunday? Then, as the unbeliever peers over the shoulders of the worshiping church it comes to her: "Surely God is in this place!"

Then, too, we fulfill the Great Commission corporately when we pray together. One man says that missionaries go out to see what God is doing in response to our prayers. Betty and I were humbled by how many people prayed specifically for us, and because of us, for Turkey. But do we have to go to a distant place to get that kind of prayer attention? Let our daily prayers for each other be missional prayers—prayers of sending out and gathering in.

In Adana I was introduced to Aykan. He has a little shop tucked away in the rabbit warren of narrow alleys in the old part of the city. He sells tea and instant coffee in bulk. When I stopped by he always offered me tea or coffee to drink (naturally!) and seemed glad to talk. I had been told that he was open to the Christian faith, but we had to be careful how we spoke in that close environment. He likes to read and I gave him some books. At last I took the risk of inviting him to our little church, and he came. It was so good to see him getting to know the different members. At last he could converse freely in his own language. He heard the gospel in the context of worship. How rich and powerful is corporate testimony. This is the "second person plural" of the Great Commission at work.

We need our buildings. Bricks and mortar tell testimony too. But let's hold them lightly. Tabernacle is a better metaphor than temple. We are just passing through. We are a pilgrim community. Pilgrims are more likely to "get out" than settlers. Sometimes, if the church gets too settled, God, in his mercy, transforms the neighbourhood. It may be easier for him to change the demographics outside the walls, than change the hearts inside! Then we become pilgrims on our own street whether we like it or not.

Buildings too can speak. Small windows and heavy doors say: "Keep out!" A small, faded sign half hidden by overgrown shrubs says: "Our welcome is reserved for insiders, who know what needs to be known without asking." When the best parking spots are "Reserved for Clergy" we betray our nostalgic world-view. Clergy privilege is part of a Christendom mentality that has long since past its best before date. It leaves a distinctly bad taste in the mouths of the not-yet churched. What message does our building send to our neighbours? Is the building there for us or for them? Does the unbeliever feel at home in our building? Is the neighbourhood as proud of our building as we are? We could try asking them.

As Christians the past is vital to us. We have a historic faith. We are rooted in specific times as well as specific places. We are neither Gnostic nor Docetic, two early movements that tried to over-spiritualize life. Churches rightly treasure their past. We love our anniversary celebrations. But let's counterbalance our pride in the past with great expectations for the future. Let's celebrate, by faith, future milestones with as much exuberance as we celebrate past milestones.

Where is that future? Here is the paradox: the future of the church is not in the church—it's out there. I love the closing words of the Latin mass, *"Ite misse est"*—"Go, the mass is finished." Or more colloquially, "That's it folks, now get out!"

....

O Lord, I am afraid of change.
Forgive me for my unbelief.
I cling to the known ways instead of clinging to you.

But this I recall to mind,
that you are the Shepherd of the whole earth
and we are the sheep of your pasture.

If we move to Turkey, you are there.
If we move to the east side of town, you are there.
If we cross the street and knock on our neighbour's door,
you are there.
If we change the order of service, you are there.

Even there your hand shall lead us
and your right hand shall hold us fast.

I pray in the name of the one who left the comfort of heaven
for the chaos of earth,
Amen.

3. Within Kissing Distance

If we do get out, how far must we go? Betty and I spent time in a distant land and a strange culture. Somehow the Lord gave us the freedom to do this. It was a great experience. But going out is not primarily about distance. We don't get brownie points for mileage. Crossing the street to visit the relatives may be a tougher challenge. But crossing over in some sense is fundamental to extending the invitation. We have to get up close and personal.

In Turkey, when men meet, they kiss each other on both cheeks. For northern European introverted types, like me, this takes some adjusting to. I like my personal space. But I had to get on with it. Otherwise there is always a question mark over you: "What's the matter with him? He doesn't like to kiss guys!" My friend Ismet always seemed to have four days worth of coarse bristle on his cheeks. When he kissed us we knew we had been kissed. We men all expressed our appreciation to him when he showed up clean shaven on Sunday mornings!

Somehow we have to get within kissing distance if we want to extend the invitation effectively.

For you are with me
There is a good, modern translation of the Bible into Turkish. It is helpful for folks like us wanting to learn the language

because the Turkish is pitched for lower level readers and the story line is familiar. As I slowly worked through Psalm 23 in Turkish for the first time, I was deeply moved as I began to feel these familiar images in this strange language. It became fresh again. When I got to verse four I wept.

Karanlık ölüm vadisinden geçsem bile,
  (Even though I walk through the valley
    of the shadow of death)
Kötülükten korkmam.
  (I will fear no evil,)
Çünkü sen benimlesin.
  (for you are with me;)
Çomağın, değneğin güven verir bana.
  (your rod and your staff, they comfort me.)

It was that third line that got me. Why am I not afraid?— "because you are with me." And just in case that sounds vague or theoretical, the poet adds the fourth line: "your rod and your staff, they comfort me." The knobbly, physical there-ness of the rod and staff "earth" that Shepherd Presence.

This is a critical point for Muslims, who, if they are devout, are consumed by the Otherness of God. They know the transcendence of God, but not the imminence of God. True, some will speak of a sense of God's closeness, but this is a kind of geographical closeness, not an emotional, or personal closeness. The idea that God would come within kissing distance is anathema to Muslims. More on this later. But Christianity is radically different at this point. What we taste in

Psalm 23 is the incarnation of God. This prayer anticipates Jesus, Immanuel, God with us.

The mystery of presence

There is great work being done with radio and satellite TV to get the message out. Literature can also be very helpful. But nothing replaces simply being there. God could have sent his message in many ways. And he did. But as the opening verse of Hebrews tells us, he didn't stop there.

> *Long ago, at many times and in many ways,*
> *God spoke to our fathers by the prophets,*
> *but in these last days he has spoken to us by his Son....*

The introduction to John's Gospel is even clearer.

> *And the Word became flesh and dwelt among us....*

Simply living close to people may be the most important thing we did in Turkey. It mirrors the incarnation of the Son of God. It puts flesh and bones on the Gospel. It brings the Word to life.

I admit, an incarnational life may be easier in a foreign country. We were strangers in their midst. We were gossiped about. We were public people, whether we liked it or not. Here in Canada we have to work harder at being present to the community. We need to move beyond just sharing the same postal code. We need face-to-face-ness. We need real presence because we need relationships. An incarnational life is a relational life.

The foundation of relationship is God himself. God is not a proposition, he is a person. He is therefore relational. He is relational within his own being. He is Trinitarian. In the West we often illustrate the Trinity with mechanical models, triangles, ice/water/steam, and so on. I like the relational models of the Eastern church. One comes from that early church leader John of Damascus. He used the word, *perichoresis* meaning "circle dance," to speak of the dynamic, joyful, interpenetrating relational life of the Trinity. Or there is the famous painting by Rublev of a table scene. The Father, Son and Holy Spirit are seated around a table delighting in each other's company. There is also an empty chair at the table. It is an invitation to us to enter into the relational life of God.

Words without relationship are throw-away words. We hit delete. Few people relish spam. And religious spam is the most disingenuous because instinctively we feel the disconnect with the character of God. God is intensely, emotionally, creatively, passionately personal. We know, because he came to visit. "We saw him, we observed him, we *touched* him," says John the apostle. He also cooked breakfast for them.

When we cross over to be present with people—in the flesh—we build connections to that Greater Presence. Nothing replaces incarnational ministry. Nothing is more compelling than a *personally* delivered invitation. Our very presence is itself an invitation.

Under the vine
We were living in Adana on the upper edge of the great Çukurova plain in southern Turkey. In July and August the city bakes under the relentless sun. We got a taste of this in the first

week of May when the temperature shot up to 37° in the shade! How do you stay cool? Our neighbours fought nature with nature. They used grape vines for shade, training them on overhead trellises in a cool, leafy canopy. What a great place to sit and drink tea and talk after the work of the day is over.

Our neighbour Yakub had a little refreshment stand conveniently located across from the gate of the high school. When business was slow, he sat under his vine in the back garden with his friend Yaşar who he had known for over forty years. I had an open invitation to join them. We were all about the same age and had a lot of fun together.

One evening I dropped by and his friend Yusuf was there. Yusuf had had a stroke that left him unable to speak. On the street some people made fun of old Yusuf, but Yakub treated him with respect, careful to speak to him as an equal. There was nothing wrong with Yusuf's hearing or his mind. I enjoyed getting to know him.

Sometimes there were five or six guys in the huddle and I couldn't keep up with the rapid fire conversation. Then Yakub would stop the show and "translate" for me. He doesn't speak a word of English but he got the point across in simplified Turkish and comical, theatrical sign language.

Sitting under a vine in the middle of Turkey talking with the neighbours—is this important in the Grand Scheme of Things? In God's grace it may well be.

Authentic presence
It is true, there are different ways of being present. Geographical presence is only the beginning. I am present to the woman at the checkout counter when I pick up milk, but

that two feet of space between us might as well be two miles. Although, even there, a friendly greeting and a name remembered can bring the encounter to life. In Turkey we looked for opportunities to make the encounter more personal. When Betty visited our neighbours she always took some family photos in her purse. As she showed pictures and talked about our children and grandchildren, she became a normal person, no longer a stranger, but "one of us." She loved her family, just as they loved theirs.

Our presence becomes more authentic when it is mutual, when it is a two-way experience. When we are present as the one holding power, it is a constricted presence. We have to get out from behind the desk. Jesus "looked up" to Zacchaeus in the tree—a rare experience for this wee little man! "Looking up to" becomes a metaphor for the humility of Jesus as he presents himself to this tax collector as one who is needy. He needs a place to stay. He is hungry. He is on the receiving end. This kind of presence is not threatening. Zacchaeus "welcomed him gladly." This powerless presence was strangely compelling. Zacchaeus suddenly "stood up" and announced a major financial cleanup. Perhaps for the first time in his life he stands tall taking ownership of his corrupt behaviour. The humble, needy, presence of Christ was transformative. "Today salvation has come to this house," said Jesus.

Our presence also becomes more authentic when it is respectful. We respect people when we value them for who they are, not for what we will turn them into! People quickly know if they are only a commodity to us. Our friendships need to be genuine. Betty's dear friend, Songül, said, "Thank you for not trying to convert us." We wrestled with that! Should we have been bolder in presenting the Gospel? We certainly prayed for them and still do. We have concluded that God delights in this friendship as much as we do. And he is not finished with us or them yet.

Our presence becomes more authentic when we acknowledge that we too are pilgrims. We are not people who have arrived. We come alongside our new friends and compare notes. We look for where they are in their pilgrimage. We do a lot of listening. We listen for what God has already been doing in their lives, and for what God will teach us through them.

Muslims think in generalizations about Christians (just as we do about Muslims). Often those generalizations are not flattering. All of the ugliest facets of the West fall under the category "Christian." My friendship with Okan at the corner store was tried and tested as a result of the Cartoon Crisis (where Mohamed was portrayed in a way that was disrespectful for Muslims). Okan was really hurting over what was, for him, a very personal matter.

For a couple of weeks I was reluctant to visit him because he would almost immediately get into a heated diatribe against the West. But our friendship pulled us through the crisis. We had drunk too many glasses of tea together. We had enjoyed each other's company too much. The particularity of our friendship broke apart the generalizations of his ideology. That can't happen without actually being there.

Corporate presence

The Bible calls the church the "body of Christ." The church, as a living community, has the potential to be a powerful, incarnational presence. This corporate presence represents

Christ much more fully than any one individual. In Adana our little church had a good relationship with the police. They showed up faithfully outside our doors on Sunday mornings, ostensibly to make sure we were not hassled by ill-wishers, though we wondered if they came primarily for our coffee and cookies. We made a point of sitting with them and getting to know their names. They seemed to enjoy coming alongside our little community. One said he planned to start attending the service after he retired. Another had two daughters who did attend. One of them eventually was baptized.

We were pushed into being present for this little group of policemen. They were literally on our doorstep. But more often it is left up to each church to decide how much they are willing to be present to the community around. In that ambiguous environment we struggled with just how open our stance should be. Safety was a concern. But even in more neutral environments churches need to be intentional about being an incarnational presence. Does our architecture breathe warmth? Some churches are using much more glass at street level as a way of expressing openness. The barrier between insider and outsider is reduced. Each is less isolated from the other.

Our corporate presence is more powerful in part because we model new and healed relationships. The more diverse the church the more compelling the witness. We visited a church where Armenians, Greeks and Turks worshiped side by side. Given the troubled history between those three groups, that shared worship was a living miracle. That church models in real time a powerfully attractive alternate reality that contrasts greatly with the hard realities of the surrounding community.

But are we willing to take the risk of welcoming those who are different? Are we willing to begin the journey towards a "Revelation 7" experience of worship? A couple of years ago in a European country we visited a church that was pure white, even though the neighbourhood was rich with colour. That church was missing a great incarnational opportunity.

The Lord does not call us out of the world. He invites us to live openly in the world, both as individuals and as churches. Yes, we have a word to speak, we have a story to tell. But that word is most powerful when it is incarnate—a word written in flesh-and-blood presence. May God grant us the grace and courage to venture within kissing distance.

... ...

Jesus said:
"As the Father has sent me, I am sending you."

...to learn their language
...to eat their food
...to drink their tea
...to wear their clothes
...to walk their streets
...to love them
...to allow them to love you
...to suffer together
...to reveal my heart
...to close the gap
...until it is no longer "they" but "us."

4. Heart Scan

We've been through too many airports in the last few years. Our luggage has been poked, prodded and x-rayed dozens of times. You would think we would know what not to pack. But luggage rules are not always consistent, and once in a while we still get caught. Sometimes we just forget something. Recently we got pulled over because of a water bottle. Out of sight, out of mind—until we tried to cross into a new area of the airport.

When we get serious about extending the invitation we realize we will have to go *in person*. It is surprising at this point how much of our hidden interior life comes to the surface as we move out of our familiar places and cross over into the unknown. We may be surprised at the inappropriate items that show up on the scanner. It is helpful to be more self-aware of our attitudes and motives before they become public.

To put a positive spin on this section, here are some thoughts on a handful of heart matters we might take on board. Maybe if we reach our weight limit with these five we won't have unwanted extras creeping in!

Adventure... check!

Betty and I spent a week traveling with one small backpack around eastern Turkey. It was not a wild, open-ended adventure (we traveled by bus, and slept in hotels), but it had its moments. It was adventurous in that we could not plan ahead very far. Certainly we had our share of the unexpected. We were stretched (figuratively speaking!) as we passed through numerous military check-points. Our limited grasp of the language meant that we often didn't understand the answer to the question we had just asked. We ended up in places we had not expected. We had only partial control over the process.

One evening we found ourselves in the little village of Çaldıran just a stone's throw from the Iranian border on the far eastern edge of Turkey. We simply got stranded there. We had planned to go further, but we discovered, too late, that the little bus we were on didn't go further, and there were no more buses that night. What to do? Then Betty spied a small hotel. It had seen better days. The water ran only intermittently and it was not as clean as we would have liked. But it was a roof over our heads. Next morning we headed north in an ancient, overloaded van, arriving a couple of hours later in Doğubeyazıt, in the shadow of Mt. Ararat.

For some of you that will sound pretty tame. Others might see it differently. Our adventure thermostats are all set at different levels. But if we are to extend the invitation we might as well enjoy the adventure. Because every time we cross over, stepping out of our circle of familiarity, we experience adventure.

Take gastronomic adventures for example. I was once asked to find and visit a certain family in Toronto. I had little money and no knowledge of the city. It was part of a mission orientation assignment. At last I found the street and knocked on the door. Before I knew it I was sitting at the table with the family, eating goat meat. This is not the time to be picky about new foods—you just dig in. A couple of years later, as we were leaving the city of Adana, the caretaker of the apartment building invited us in for a last meal. As we sat down on the floor to eat in the traditional way (they come from a mountain village) we were love-bound to eat whatever was put in front of us, with relish. We still don't know what we ate!

It's often the simple things, like new foods, that test our sense of adventure. Or toilets. Squat toilets are still common in Turkey. The guys have it easier at this point. But we all quickly learn to carry our own toilet paper. Then there is life on the street. We have to quickly adjust to new traffic rules if we are to survive. If we struggle against everything that is not exactly the we way it was where we grew up we will be emotionally drained all the time.

So as we extend the invitation and move out across the boundaries of what is familiar to us, a sense of adventure is vital. Expect the unexpected. In new environments the things we plan seldom work out as projected, because there are new variables we could not have anticipated. There are new ways of doing almost everything, not to mention new ways of being.

Adventure and risk are near cousins. But the more we know our Heavenly Father the more we are at home in his world. He knows what we can handle. He is not out to nail us. We don't mind tweaking the adventure thermostat up a notch when we are convinced that underneath are the "everlasting arms."

And as we ride the wave, sometimes more out of control than we would like, doors unexpectedly open. Two years after eating that goat meat in Toronto, that same family tracked us down and began supporting us financially. And out there on the far eastern border of Turkey we met a warm and friendly village imam who accepted a New Testament from us.

Respect... check!

If we are going to extend the invitation, a deep sense of respect for the other person is essential. Respect is not an optional extra. I like the old Quaker perspective: respect is "Answering that of God in every person." When we are convinced that every person we meet is made in the image of God, we will value them, we will treasure them, we will encounter them with a sense of awe, we will respect them. We will value each one in their own right, not as a project but as a person.

When we respect people we will speak of them the same way in private as we do to their face. We will not succeed in extending the invitation if our so-called respect is just a role we assume for outreach. Real respect has only one face. Courtesy is the culturally shaped outward form of respect. We can fake courtesy, but we can't fake respect. People will know. Deep calls to deep.

Jesus says, "I stand at the door and knock." Really? If anyone has the right to just walk in, it is the Lord Jesus Christ. But he waits to be invited. He respects the other-ness of us creatures. When the two blind men stopped Jesus on the road to Jerusalem he didn't just assume he knew what they wanted. "What do you want me to do for you?" he asked. Such a respectful encounter. He had time for them in the middle of an intense, crowded schedule.

Perhaps respect is really about how the other weighs in relation to ourselves. If other people weigh little, we will attend to them less, especially when we are in the middle of something that is important to us.

We are respectful when we promote the good in other people at least as much as we do in ourselves. I get tired of people who seem to make a career of pointing out the negative aspects of another group. We wondered why certain folk came to Turkey. At least they provoked me to broadcast good news stories: A trained medical rescue team of three doctors, two nurses and one health official were sent by the Yeni Yüksektepe Cultural Association to the Philippines to help with a mudslide disaster... On May 15th, 2007 Elif Maviş became the first Turkish woman to reach the top of Mount Everest....

We think our attitudes are neatly packed out of sight, but we are scanned before we know it and the secrets of the heart are public. As we venture out to extend the invitation we realize the only genuine invitation is a respectful invitation.

Love... check!

With strange foods, tolerance is enough. Betty and I never did get to like olives, and there we were living in the land of olives. At least we could tolerate them. With strange people, however, toleration is not enough. We have to move beyond tolerance to acceptance, and beyond acceptance to affirmation, and beyond affirmation to appreciation then delight. This is love.

Yes, Christian love is a verb. It is active. It is sacrificial. It is about working for the best for another. But that is still pretty watery soup if we don't begin to enjoy being with the other person. It's too easy to say, "I don't like him, but I love him." I think Jesus enjoyed his time with the twelve. It wasn't all deep and serious. Surely a chuckle went round the group when Jesus came up with the nickname "Thunder-boys" for James and John. When we share smiles and laughter we leap-frog from duty to delight. May God help us move on from a scripted, paint-by-numbers kind of love, to a bluesy, jazzy, improvised, from the heart, splash-of-passion, kind of love.

Well, OK, at least we can begin to stretch in that direction. Let's be realistic, some people are harder to love. It is hard to think sweet thoughts about the guy that just stole your wallet. And sometimes people just seem so foreign and different that we wonder if we could ever love them. But we can.

I remember a time when I looked across the street at a certain group of people and they all looked the same. How do their mothers tell them apart? Now I can hardly believe I thought that way. Each has a name and a face and a history— Murat, Oğzhan, Orhan, Ahmet, Sait—each with his unique personality. The generic "them" and "they" has dropped from my vocabulary as it should.

What is the shortcut past fear and prejudice? It is simply to get to know the other. Spend time together. Listen. Invite him into your home. Visit his place. Work on a project together. Find out what her gifts are and ask for help. Find out what her need is and offer a hand. Sometimes this works best when the church is involved as a community. Often it has to begin one on one.

Perhaps we find it hard to love because we are trying to love generically, we are trying to love anonymously. But it doesn't work that way. Love is relational. Love is face specific. It is particular. It seems risky, but we have to reach across the gap and begin a conversation. Knowing comes before loving.

Hope... check!

Did you ever notice that there are *two* commissions at the end of Matthew's Gospel. First the soldiers are commissioned to proclaim a dead Jesus. Then the disciples are commissioned to proclaim a living Jesus.

Without good quality hope in our pockets we will get stuck at that first commission. That first commission is our default setting. At least the pay is good. And the working conditions are much better. Stiff opposition lies ahead for those who are determined to fulfill the greater commission. The world, the flesh and the devil conspire against us.

Good quality, serviceable hope is essential mission equipment because extending the invitation can be discouraging. One man said, "You can plant three churches in twelve years in Turkey and not have to change buildings." How do you fix the revolving door? And if you get it fixed will it last? We poured ten years of our lives into a small, country church in eastern Canada—Bible classes, Sunday school, prayer meetings, choir practice, laughter, tears and worship. Today no sign remains of that building and the remnant flock is scattered. Our hope better be durable.

Hope is a word that badly needs refurbishing. For most of us now the word hope is about as inspiring as a wet paper bag: "I hope I can find a job, but...."

Is it possible to revive New Testament hope—that protective, armour-plated, hard-as-a-helmet kind of hope (1 Thessalonians 5:8)? New Testament hope is more like "expectation," or "anticipation." It is solid, we can count on it, the foundation has already been laid, completion is assured— God has given us his word that it will be so.

And that's the key. We will *hope* again when we *believe* again. When we believe that God's Word really is God's Word, our hope will not be shaken.

We have this as a sure and steadfast anchor of the soul,
a hope that enters into the inner place behind the curtain,
where Jesus has gone as a forerunner on our behalf
having become a high priest forever...
Hebrews 6:19-20

Keep a firm grip on the promises. They are very precious. Ephesians 5:25-27 tells us that one day, we the church will be spotlessly clean and wrinkle-free. Is God able to do this? The apostle Paul is pretty confident: "And I am sure of this, that he who began a good work in you will bring it to completion at the day of Jesus Christ" (Philippians 1:6). And it doesn't hurt to look regularly at that snapshot God keeps on his desk—his "preferred future." Here it is again:

After this I looked, and behold,
a great multitude that no one could number,
from every nation, from all tribes and peoples and languages,
standing before the throne and before the Lamb...
Revelation 7:9

Boldness... check!
Boldness is tricky. Some boldness is out of place. "Don't be bold," says the mother to the child. Some boldness conveys arrogance. But when we begin to extend the invitation good boldness is essential equipment. It is easy to be timid about

offering that Bible when, as a Christian, you are out-numbered 50,000 to one. Even in the Bible Belt it takes guts to invite the neighbour to Alpha. We are not the first believers to feel this. Here is the Church's first recorded prayer request: "And now, Lord, look upon their threats and grant to your servants to continue to speak your Word with all boldness" (Acts 4:29).

This "boldness" is an important theme in the New Testament. It is not just raw courage. It is a certain kind of courage. It is courage for speaking—and more specifically, for speaking the Gospel.

Where does this boldness come from? The boys from the Sanhedrin were astonished at the boldness of Peter and John as they preached the gospel. They were obviously uneducated, so that wasn't the source of their boldness. Then they remembered—"they had been with Jesus" (Acts 4:13). Boldness is the birthright of the children of God. But, like all God's gifts, we have to receive it and unwrap it and hit the start button.

Muslims typically come to Christ slowly. It takes years of building relationships with the Word percolating gently in the background. If God allows us to be part of this process we need patience. Yet there are moments of opportunity. Then we must seize our gift of boldness and walk through the door. After all the time we spent with Songül and family there did come a right time to give them a Bible. When Ahmet, literally in the shadow of the mosque, in that very public tea room, wanted to know more about the gospel, I had to push timidity aside.

What about those people who are naturally bold, or come from bold cultures? They too need to hear this. Natural boldness is often a hindrance. This New Testament boldness is a spiritual boldness. Both the naturally bold and the naturally timid must take it up.

Sometimes the bold speaking is directed upwards in prayer. In fact we are invited to pray this way: "Let us then with confidence [boldness] draw near to the throne of grace, that we may receive mercy and find grace to help in time of need" (Hebrews 4:16). As my friendship with Yakub deepened I began to get more insistent with God, even angry. "Lord, don't you care about my friend? Don't you see what a character he is? Heaven will be a dull place without him. Do something!" Within a couple of days he had asked me for a Bible. And so my good Muslim friend began reading the Word of God in public on the side of the street telling his family and his friends what he was discovering. And he could speak the language! God was evidently not offended by my in-his-face prayer.

A sense of adventure, a deep respect for people, a willingness to love particular individuals, a firm grip on hope, a healthy boldness—this will get us started.

....

O Lord, I am afraid of chasing people away.
Search me, O God, and know my heart!

Try me and know my thoughts!
Scan me and see if there is any offensive way in me...

Is there any way you can speed up the sanctification process?
—if not for my sake, at least for the sake of my new friends?

I pray in the name of the one who never crushed a broken spirit
(though he did whip up a nice storm in the temple!)
Amen

5. The Way We Do Things Around Here

In Adana we were surprised by culture. About twice a month we went with our British friends to the city theater to enjoy the local, seventy piece, symphony orchestra. They were good, often accompanying world-class soloists. We always got front-row balcony seats—no safety rail to impede the view—and soaked in the experience. We couldn't afford not to be cultured with tickets at five dollars.

We can't talk about extending the invitation without talking about culture. But we are not talking here about listening to classical music. We might call that Adana experience "high culture." Here we are thinking about culture in its more generic sense. The simplest definition I have heard is this: "Culture is the way we do things around here." True, culture is a way of *being* as well as a way of *doing*, but we encounter culture first in its outward expression.

Culture is not just something we think about overseas. One of the side benefits of our venture into the missionary experience was that Betty and I had the privilege of visiting many different churches here in Canada. We soon discovered that each church has its own distinct culture. The nine-o'clock service at one church was free-flowing, unstructured, un-tied and contemporary. The eleven-o'clock service at the next church was liturgical, robed, choreographed and punctual. Each speaking engagement was another cross-cultural experience for us.

We are all children of our own culture. We are profoundly shaped by our culture. But usually we are unaware of our own culture. It is just the way we do things around here. We are immersed in it like fish in the sea. It is all we have ever known. It is so much a part of us that it is invisible to us. We cannot imagine any other way of doing things. It is not a topic of conversation because there is no need to talk about it. This is who we are.

Then we encounter another culture. And we suddenly realize we don't know the rules. We don't know whether to stand or sit. We don't know what to call people. We don't know what is appropriate or inappropriate. We suddenly become self-conscious. Many people don't understand the grammar of their own language well until they start to learn another language. In the same way, as we encounter other cultures we begin to understand ourselves more fully.

We need to talk about culture because extending the invitation will take us to different cultures. The culture of Judea is different from the culture of Jerusalem. The culture of Samaria is different from the culture of Judea. The culture of the "uttermost part of the earth" is utterly different from all of the above. Imagine a country where the workers go on strike by working so hard that the increase in production shames the employers into giving an increase in pay!

We need to talk about culture because expectations are different in different cultures. What is appropriate in one culture is inappropriate in another. Take time, for example.

Some cultures are clock oriented. These people take great pride in things starting on time. Punctuality is valued highly. Other cultures are event-oriented. Meetings begin when everyone is present. Relationships take priority. It is more important to see that everyone is there than to start at a specific time. One way to unpack time values is to ask: How late is too late? Answers vary from half a minute to half an hour or more. If everyone is on the same cultural page you don't even think about the issue. But imagine the fun in a multi-cultural congregation!

When we are reading off different cultural scripts it is helpful if we are more self conscious about our own value systems and more understanding of the values of others. As we become culturally literate humour displaces irritability.

The group vs. the individual

One helpful way to get at the culture question is to ask: Are these people group-oriented or individual-oriented? The Western world tends to be more individualistic, the rest of the world more group oriented.

What does this mean? Well, consider child-raising. Western parents see their new-born children as dependant beings. The goal of child-raising is to teach them to be independent—"to stand on their own two feet." Non-Western parents see this quite differently. The child is born with no knowledge of how to relate properly to others. The goal of child-raising is to teach the child how to "fit in"—to know his or her place in the group.

Imagine the crosscurrents in the nursery of the multicultural church. The Western-culture parents are embarrassed when their child is "clingy" and doesn't like being left alone while the parents attend the service. The non-Western parents may find it impossible to leave their child with strangers. They either sit at the back of the church holding their baby, or crowd into the nursery alongside the appointed care-givers.

Whose cultural agenda sets the rules of child care in the church? Who holds power? Does our child-care policy help or hinder our attempts to extend the invitation? If hospitality is only extended on our terms it is not genuine hospitality.

Or think about the concept of personal space. We Westerners like privacy. We like our own rooms with doors that have locks. Non-Western homes are typically much more open. There is little privacy. Most space is shared space. There isn't the need or desire to be alone. In Turkey people love to get together in the evenings just to talk and hang out. Our neighbours no doubt thought it strange that we would often be home alone in the evenings. But we needed to recharge our Western made batteries.

Language also holds clues as to the importance of the group. For example Turkish has many words denoting relationships. There is one word for brother. There is another for older brother. A younger brother must always address his older brother with the correct term. In the same way I would never call my language teacher simply by his first name. He is Mahmut *hoca* (teacher). My older friend is Sait *amca* (uncle). Turkish is a language of respect.

In group cultures individual identity is shaped by the group. You are who you are in relation to the group. Yes, people are still unique individuals, but they are, as the anthropologists say, "like an egg without the shell." Think of the trauma of conversion for such people. It will likely mean being wrenched from their group. This will tear at their very identity. Who am I apart from my group? How can I stand alone? It is important for them to be warmly embraced by the church. The church will be their new community, and they will find their new identity in the context of this new family of God.

Honour-shame orientation

Imagine visiting a jewelry store. You are fascinated by the beauty of the gems in their finely crafted settings. In a moment of weakness you slip a ring into your pocket and walk out. Later, sitting at home, admiring the ring, you are suddenly overcome with guilt. You have committed an act of theft. It is wrong to steal.

Then you switch on the TV and to your horror you discover that there was a security camera in the jewelry store and the film of you stealing that ring is being shown on the six-o-clock news. As you think about your friends and family seeing this you are now not only suffering from guilt, you are also overwhelmed with shame.

What is the difference between guilt and shame? Guilt is about breaking a law. Shame is about being *seen* to have broken a law. It is about being seen negatively by those whose opinion you care about. Guilt is about breach of principle. Shame is about breach of relationship. Guilt is about what I did. Shame is about who I am. Guilt is about stealing. Shame is about being a thief. Guilt is about activity. Shame is about identity.

All people deal with both guilt and shame, but group cultures are more shame-oriented. In group cultures people are who they are in the eyes of others, thus shame is much closer to the surface. Shame is about being seen negatively by the group. Honour is the other side of the coin. Honour is the positive assessment of the group. Honour and shame are powerful forces in group cultures.

So group-oriented people are much more concerned about "losing face" (being shamed, or dishonoured) than individual-oriented people. At the church business meeting of the multi-cultural church the group-oriented people find it difficult to participate. To debate publicly is too risky. The vote is unanimously in favour—but don't kid yourself! Roberts Rules of Order don't work for group-oriented people. When we are serious about extending the invitation we will look for ways of doing church that are less exclusively Western.

We will also think about how we present the Gospel to shame-oriented people. We are expert at presenting the Gospel as grace for guilt. As Westerners we have read the Gospel through our guilt-oriented cultural spectacles. But for many people guilt is not the issue, shame is the issue. For them the question is not: What is the good news for guilt? The question is: What is the good news for shame?

Jesus wasn't a white guy

Jesus never did pull up his chair to the table and sit down to eat a meal of meat and potatoes with a knife and fork. He didn't drink tea or coffee. He didn't wear pants or shirts or ties. When his accusers tried to shame him he skillfully defended his honour, as a true Middle Easterner, to the delight of the crowds. He was protective of his Father's honour. He had a heart for those who lived a shamed life on the margin of the community. Jesus was not born a Westerner. He was incarnate in a group-oriented culture, an honour-shame culture. This shaped him to the core of his being. He inhabited a very different social and psychological world than we do. If Jesus had emigrated to Canada he would have experienced profound culture shock.

One of the great blessings that comes from being more self-conscious about culture is the realization that Bible culture is not Western culture. Bible culture is Middle Eastern culture, it is group culture, and it is honour-shame culture. The blessing comes especially from a deeper understanding of the life and ministry of Jesus. We begin to understand how much the ministry of Christ meant to shame-oriented people. We even find the Gospel speaking to hungry corners of our own souls that were not touched by our traditional Western gospel presentations.

Grace for guilt is unmerited forgiveness. Grace for shame is unmerited acceptance. Where we were once seen negatively, we are now seen positively. The metaphors of adoption, inclusion, citizenship, welcome, embrace, etc., are helpful in expressing the good news for shame-oriented people. And when this language is lived out, embodied, it is powerful. Jesus welcomed the shamed. He took their shame to himself and bore their shame on the cross. The Gospel of Jesus welcomes the shamed into the Kingdom of God and grants a fresh deposit of honour. In the family of God those who were nobodies become somebodies. May we who are the body of Christ make present to the world the whole Gospel of Christ.

Cultural calisthenics

The mission experts talk about becoming 150% culture people. We try to pull back from our own culture. At the same time we stretch forward into the target culture. This is no easy matter. We are deeply embedded in our own culture. We take it in with our mothers' milk. In so many areas of our life we are simply unaware of how much we are shaped by our own culture. We struggle to accept that other ways of being are even possible.

But we need to stretch. It is not reasonable to expect "them" to be like "us," whoever "they" are. At the very least lets try to meet in the middle. We stretch across cultural gaps because this is what Christ has done for us. We build bridges because this is what Christ did for us. We study to learn a new cultural language.

As we extend the invitation across greater cultural distances we discover something very precious. Multi-cultural fellowship is much richer than mono-cultural fellowship. People of other cultures see new sides of God. They see things we miss, just as we see things they miss. God is glorified and honoured more fully in a diverse congregation. We discover new depths to the meaning of unity in Christ. Unity based on sameness is thin. Unity based on Christ is rich.

. . . .

Thank you Lord Jesus for my new friends.

Even if I can't understand their jokes,
Even if I can't figure them out most of the time.

We are brothers and sisters—your Spirit has made us one.

We smile when we see each other on the street.
In worship our hearts sing together in harmony.

Thank you for stretching across to me in my little white house.
One day I will understand your Middle Eastern jokes,
Amen

6. Unwritten House Rules

When we lived in Vancouver we took in international students. Betty wrote up a list of house rules. It is helpful for everyone when we clarify expectations. But in reality, what we get down on paper is only the tip of the iceberg. Most of our patterns of behaviour seem as normal to us as breathing. It would never occur to us to put them on paper. Things like how we greet each other, or where we sit, or who is important. In our churches the most significant rules are not written in the bylaws. Its just the way we do things around here.

In this section I want to talk more specifically about these kinds of practical cultural differences—the unwritten house rules. We don't want to come across as cultural bumpkins when we extend the invitation to our Muslim neighbours.

Hospitality

I went to say goodbye to my friend Okan at the lamp shop before leaving Istanbul to join Betty for two weeks in Canada. It was about two-thirty in the afternoon when I dropped in, but there he was, getting ready to eat a late lunch. With typical Eastern hospitality he insisted I join him—and how could I refuse!

Okan spread a clean sheet of newspaper over the little table. He cut up a tomato and a cucumber, sliced some cheese, and put some olives in a dish. Then, like a magician, he reached into an old kettle and pulled out two hard boiled eggs. We sat down and he picked up the loaf of bread, broke it in two, and gave me half, and we began to eat.

I asked Okan about that second egg. What he expecting someone? He replied: "We Muslims are always ready to receive visitors. Guests are a gift from God."

We learned a lot about hospitality from our Muslim neighbours. We arrived as strangers, not speaking the language, suspected (rightly!) of having a hidden religious agenda, yet we were warmly welcomed into so many homes. We were treated as family, greeted with a kiss on both cheeks, made to feel special. We hope we will be more gracious in our hospitality in the future than we have been in the past, especially to the stranger in our midst. Hospitality is part of Middle Eastern culture generally. For Muslims in particular, if you don't offer hospitality, you are no better than a pagan.

But it is not enough to *value* hospitality. We have to learn the *language* of hospitality. Good intentions alone are inadequate. We must express hospitality in a way that connects. We need to learn what it takes to be heard.

One Turkish woman returned from her time in Canada complaining about the lack of hospitality there. In reality she had often been invited, but she always said no. Back in Turkey it was inappropriate to seem too eager to accept an invitation. Within her own culture everyone knew this and asked two or three times, pressing home the invitation. Then it was safe to say "Yes." When her Canadian friends took her "No" at face value, she assumed they didn't really want her company even though she longed to join them. We have to learn to extend the invitation in a way that communicates in the cultural context.

What has been our experience of being a guest? First we are warmly greeted at the door. *"Hoşgeldiniz!*—Welcome!" The whole household crowds around. It would be rude for someone to just continue what they are doing when guests arrive. This would be dishonouring to the whole household, and being hospitable is about acting honourably.

Cleanliness has a high value in Muslim culture. One way this is expressed is in distinguishing inside from outside. The inside of the house is kept spotlessly clean. For us as guests this means leaving our shoes outside the door. We are immediately offered slippers from the large supply. We are careful to step into them across the threshold and not track dirt into the house. But the gracious host will usually then offer to bring the shoes in for safekeeping, putting them just inside the door.

It is important to greet each person in the room as you enter, whether you know them or not. This feels awkward in a larger group, say at church. But this is not the time for false modesty. It is polite and respectful to recognize each person. Not to greet someone would be taken as a slight, though they would work hard at not showing it. I wonder what will happen to this rule as churches grow larger. Certainly in the home the greeting is important.

Turkish society is still a civil society. There are customs and practices to be observed. There are appropriate things to say at the appropriate time. There is an etiquette. Some of this only works in the Turkish language. For example when you put food or drink in front of someone you say *"Affiyet olsun."* We don't have this in English, but it is similar to the French *"Bon appetit."*

Much of the etiquette relates to behaviour. For example it is not polite to slouch in the chair. It is a sign of disrespect. Sit up straight. Don't sit with your back to others. People are much less likely to cross their legs, possibly because of the risk of pointing the sole of your foot at someone (considered impolite). The guest of honour sits furthest from the door (the place, supposedly, of greatest safety).

Mealtime

It is important not to arrive too early in the evening, unless you have been specifically invited for a meal. Turks eat later than we normally do in Canada, seven or eight o'clock or after. If you arrive at meal time they will be obligated to serve you a meal also. Even if you do avoid the mealtime you may have to refuse a number of times the insistent offer of food. This is the good host being polite.

If you are invited for a meal it is not polite to seem too eager at the table. Don't reach for food. This makes the host feel ashamed for not noticing that your plate is empty. In fact the host will put food on your plate unasked. He or she will insist that you keep eating, assuming that your reticence is simply politeness. It is rude for the host to allow your plate or cup to remain empty. You will probably have to leave some food on the plate to stem the flow. It is not easy to lose weight in this environment!

It is a great privilege to be invited to eat with a family. It sends a deep message. You are one of us, you are accepted, you belong, what is mine is now yours. Meals are not hurried. This is a time for talk. There is much laughter and respectful bantering. The guest praises the quality of the food. The host says it is nothing. It is a kind of dance as people slowly get to know each other. Nothing is rushed.

Muslims, like Jews, have dietary laws. And some will insist on eating only *halal* foods. But for the average Muslim these dietary laws are boiled down to the one basic rule: Thou shalt not eat pork. Obviously when we visit others we simply eat what is put in front of us. But it is important to be aware of the no pork rule when inviting people in. When Muslim friends asked us what kind of farming we did we responded discretely. No need for our past life as hog-producers to come between us. We focused on the garden, the chickens and the cattle.

After the main meal we were usually ushered into another room to sit in softer chairs and relax. On a hot summer evening we might sit up on the roof or out on the balcony. After a few minutes tea is brought. We are not asked if we want tea. If the guest is asked the polite answer would be no. Everyone knows this and it would call into question the sincerity of the host. So tea and dessert are simply brought. Dessert is often a selection of fruit. In more Westernized homes we might be offered cake. The tea glasses are refilled as often as we empty them until at last we surrender and place our spoons politely upside down across the top.

It is important not to rush off too quickly after a meal. Relax. Drink tea. Get to know each other. Give warning before you leave. Announce that you are leaving. The host will politely insist that you stay. The night is still young, etc. A little while later you again announce it is time you were off. Again the polite insistence to stay. Usually by the third announcement it is safe to stand and politely but firmly head towards the door.

At the door the host will put your shoes ready and hold your coat. They will insist you come again. *"Bekliyoruz—we are waiting!"* Often we were accompanied to the bus stop. Or at least they waited at the door and waved until we were out of sight. Sometimes we received a phone call to see if we had arrived home safely. One family insisted on driving us home. In this way guests are honoured and cared for.

Relationships matter
Of course the outward patterns of etiquette can easily become artificial. Turks often laugh at themselves in this and quickly see through the façade. But the etiquette does reflect a deep respect for people. Relationships are important to them and their society has developed outward forms to convey that.

Even if we have not yet learned all the finer points of how to behave, if we have a respectful attitude, that will cover many gaps. What is important is a sincere regard for the other person. This means being willing to offer the gift of time. Nothing conveys disrespect like rushing in and out. In Turkey there is no artificial distinction between quality time and quantity time. Quality means quantity.

This slower pace cuts across many areas of life. When shopping it is better to take a little time. An abrupt, "How much is that?" will not build bridges and only confirms negative stereotypes. Even when picking up a newspaper it doesn't hurt to exchange a greeting. When shopping for larger items, like furniture, we made a point of talking first. Where are you from (your hometown)? How about family? How long have you been selling here? After all, for us too, getting to know this person is more important than buying the item. In any case we would rather buy from a friend than a stranger.

Gender
Back in Canada I went to the barbershop and found myself getting a haircut from a woman. This would never happen in Turkey. I had a pointed moment of cultural readjustment—a strange woman was touching my head!

It is hard to know how much gender roles in Turkey are shaped by Islam and how much they simply reflect traditional Middle Eastern culture that we read about, for example, in the Old Testament. What we see is a sharper divide between male and females roles and space than we are used to in Western life. Maleness and femaleness seem more deeply etched. Men occupy public space. Women occupy private space. Men spend time with men, women with women. Retired men often have some little income generating scheme—running a little store, polishing shoes on the sidewalk, or selling items off a portable stand—but this may be as much about filling the need for an acceptable male role as it is about fund-raising. It wouldn't do for the retired man to hang around the house with the women.

Part of the separation of the sexes is about maintaining sexual purity. The honour of the family is at stake here. It is not enough to be pure, you must be seen to be pure. There must be no reason for tongues to start wagging. Thus, traditionally, women dress modestly, elbows and knees are covered, necklines are high, clothing is lose. In some families the women not only cover their hair while outside the home, but inside too when visitors come.

We outsiders must be alert to this dynamic. Only women may enter the house if the man is not at home. When we do visit as a couple we are aware that some women are uncomfortable even shaking hands with a man. Women may be uncomfortable eating with men they don't know well. Direct eye contact between men and women must be brief or it will quickly convey romantic interest. We don't want to send unintended signals! Men should direct their attention mainly to the husband when talking to a couple. In general women visit back and forth among themselves in their homes. Men meet together out of the house in the public arena.

This doesn't mean that Muslim couples can't have a warm relationship. Betty's friend Songül and her husband Rıfat are devout Muslims. In his retirement Rıfat became chair of the counsel at the local mosque. But on Valentine's day he came home with a red blouse for his wife (in the right size!) And for Mother's day he always writes a poem for her. She proudly showed us her collection from previous years. We often saw couples walking arm in arm down the street in the cool of the evening chatting away.

The power distribution between the sexes is not easy to discern. Out on the street men call the shots. But how much of that is for appearance—a thin veneer of patriarchy for public consumption? Nature has a way of balancing things out. We once saw Songül tell her husband in no uncertain terms that he had to go out on the balcony to smoke. Mothers and grandmothers are held in high regard and have a lot of influence over the family. Many women are well educated in Turkey.

On the one hand men present to the world a tough, macho front. The average Turkish man dresses conservatively, keeps his hair in good trim, sports a moustache, smokes a cigarette and walks tall. On the other hand men show a lot of affection between themselves. The kiss on each cheek is a warm welcome, not just a formality. Men will sit close together when talking, often one has a hand on the other's knee or shoulder. When Sait and I went for our prayer walks around the park in Adana he would take me by the arm—something else I had to adjust to.

As we extend the invitation over larger cultural distances we discover many more ways of getting into trouble! It is true, love and real respect cover over a multitude of cultural sins; nevertheless, surely it is better for us to make an effort to learn the new script and not stumble over our lines.

Here is a classic Middle-Eastern scenario to practice on. What non-Western cultural moments do you see in the passage below from Genesis 18?

> *And the Lord appeared to him [Abraham] by the oaks of Mamre, as he sat at the door of his tent in the heat of the day. He lifted up his eyes and looked, and behold, three men were standing in front of him.*
>
> *When he saw them, he ran from the tent door to meet them and bowed himself to the earth and said, "O Lord, if I have found favor in your sight, do not pass by your servant. Let a little water be brought, and wash your feet, and rest yourselves*

under the tree, while I bring a morsel of bread, that you may refresh yourselves, and after that you may pass on—since you have come to your servant." So they said, "Do as you have said."

And Abraham went quickly into the tent to Sarah and said, "Quick! Three seahs of fine flour! Knead it, and make cakes." And Abraham ran to the herd and took a calf, tender and good, and gave it to a young man, who prepared it quickly. Then he took curds and milk and the calf that he had prepared, and set it before them.

And he stood by them under the tree while they ate.

7. Listening to the Muslim Heart

There is a story that Francis of Assisi tried to stop the fifth crusade by walking overland through enemy lines to speak personally with Malik al-Kamil, sultan of Egypt. It was a tremendous display of courage and humility. That powerful Muslim leader responded by saying: "If all Christians were like you, Francis, all Muslims should become Christians."

Francis offered a powerful alternative to the triumphalist approach of the crusades. This alternative is needed just as much, if not more so, on the present international stage. We have now a remarkable opportunity to bear the name of Christ in the spirit of Christ. Can we be present with our Muslim friends, both in our Canadian neighbourhoods and overseas, with respect and humility as well as godly boldness? It is time to wage peace not war.

Beyond the six o' clock news

If we are going to extend the invitation to our Muslim neighbours we must move beyond a "news clip" image of Islam. We need a larger picture. We need perspective. We need Muslim friends. There are seventy million Muslims in Turkey. Almost all of them are ordinary folk getting on with life as best they can, trying to get their kids to school on time, worrying about their credit card payments, forgetting to pick up the milk on the way home from work. We will begin to move beyond our hatred of Islam when we discover we love and respect someone who also happens to be Muslim.

This works two ways. Our Muslim neighbours see the Christian West through their own lenses. For Muslims the crusades are not distant history, they feel as though they happened yesterday. The invasion of Iraq is just the latest manifestation of the crusades. The relentless march of Western commercialism and secularism is a more subtle, but even more powerful crusading presence. There are now ninety Starbucks outlets in Turkey.

Muslims watch all this nervously. They are horrified at the possibility their children might become Christians. They will become secularized. They will lose their family values and their respect for elders. Divorce rates will soar. The Christian West doesn't look very attractive to faithful Muslims. Muslims will begin to move beyond their hatred of Christianity when they discover they love and respect someone who also happens to be Christian.

Not a secular world

When we moved from Canada to Turkey we moved from a secular world to a religious world. It is far easier to talk publicly about Christianity in Turkey than in Canada. (Try sharing the Gospel at the neighbourhood coffee shop!) In Turkey religion is often the third topic of conversation after the weather and, "Where are you from?"

Faithful Muslims live life under the eye of a creator God. They pray. Songül heard that our daughter was sick. She told us later, "I pray for her five times a day."

I enjoyed visiting the mosque in our neighbourhood of Istanbul. It isn't a tourist destination, just a typical working mosque. The structure itself is only about twenty years old, but like most Turkish mosques it is built in the traditional Ottoman style. My friend Ahmet shows me around. The building is immaculately maintained. It is a place of prayer and we take off our shoes as we enter and speak in low voices. It is cool and airy under a high, beautifully painted dome. The sunlight is filtered and softened through stained glass windows. After the non-stop hustle of the street the quietness is refreshing. Three men are praying silently.

Islam is a kind of public monasticism. Prayer is interwoven with the rest of life, worship and world are not separated, the place of prayer lies adjacent to the place of work. Architecturally this means the mosque is often part of the streetscape with shops and restaurants around and underneath. I met Ahmet at the book shop under the mosque. Once a week, on Fridays, we got together at the little tea room next door and practiced Turkish and English together until the late afternoon call to prayer took him upstairs.

Prayer reminds us that we are not God, we are created beings. Muslims are very aware of the holiness of God. You don't have to tell Muslims that they don't measure up to that holiness. They already have a deep sense of their own unworthiness. We Westerners assume we merit salvation; Muslims assume they don't. They look only to God's mercy. Our challenge is to accept that we *need* mercy. Their challenge is to accept that God *offers* mercy.

Of course many Muslims have only a nominal faith. And many others mix Islam with superstition and magic. Some students of Islam estimate that about eighty percent of Muslims practice some kind of syncretistic Folk Islam. Even after converting to Christ it may take a while to wash away the remnants of magical practice and thinking.

I was talking with Apti, a Christian brother. He was asking for prayers for his girlfriend who had been giving him the cold shoulder. Another fellow, Veysi, a new-comer to the church, half jokingly suggested he use a spell. I say half jokingly because spells and curses are used a lot in Turkey. Fortunately a pastor who was also with us was able to clarify, in no uncertain terms, and in clear Turkish, that we who follow Jesus have no part in these techniques.

This corrupt, syncretistic version of Islam holds many people in deep bondage. It feeds a life of fear, anxiety and suspicion. This is something to keep in the back of our minds as we meet our Muslim neighbours. How wonderful it is to walk in the freedom that Christ gives. More incentive to reach across and begin a transforming friendship.

The person of Christ
I enjoy getting to know faithful Muslims, like Okan. Earlier I only told you half of the story of my impromptu lunch with him at the lamp shop. As he picked up the loaf of bread, broke it in two, and gave me half, I was deeply moved as his action reminded me of the communion feast. It seemed only right to pray.

So I held my hands out, palms up, in the Muslim way, and prayed a simple prayer of thanks. My first (very short!) public

Turkish prayer. Okan seemed to appreciate it. There was a third chair at the table, empty. In my heart I asked the Lord Jesus to join us, but of course he was there before me. Okan and I talked about the weather and about our families. He asked about my trip and how long it would take. We laughed about some little thing. Two good friends enjoying lunch together. Then, as we finished, Okan lifted his hands and gave an end-of-meal prayer of thanks.

Sometimes I felt spiritually close to Okan. We both turned our hearts to the one true God, the Maker of heaven and earth, the final Judge. At other times I realized we were far apart. Earlier I had told him about the birth of our new granddaughter. He asked me, with a grin, if I realized that all babies are born Muslims. Naturally I protested. So she was born a Christian then? Again I protested. I tried to say something about our "broken hearts" in my limited Turkish. But he scoffed at the idea that children have any sin before the age of twelve or thirteen. In such moments I realized how far apart we were in our understanding of sin and redemption and our need for a saviour.

This brings us to the heart of the matter in the conversation between Islam and Christianity. The great question is, "Who is Christ?" Muslims honour Christ as a prophet. They even believe he will return one day. But for them he is not Immanuel. He is not "God with us." For Muslims God is totally Other. It is impossible for him to be "with us" in that sense. Muslims know the transcendence of God—perhaps better than we do. But they do not know the immanence of God. They do not know Jesus. And because they reject Jesus they do not know God as they might. It is in the face of Jesus that we see God most clearly.

> *For God, who said, "Let light shine out of darkness,"*
> *has shone in our hearts*
> *to give the light of the knowledge of the glory of God*
> *in the face of Jesus Christ (2 Corinthians 4:6).*

After I spoke more explicitly to Okan about Christ, our relationship changed. We were not as close. Christ either unites us or divides us. But while there is life there is hope. We haven't seen the last chapter yet in Okan's life.

Conversion as process

For most Muslims who convert to Christ the experience is more process than event. A seven year conversion process is not exceptional. My language teacher Mahmut took thirty years from his first contact to the time of his baptism. It is not hard to see why. Conversion touches every area of the Muslim's life.

Islam does not compartmentalize the world. There is no separation of church and state. Islam incorporates all of life. This is one reason why conversion is so difficult, why it takes so much time, and why it is so traumatic. Conversion is seen as a betrayal of country, culture and clan. It is an abandonment of a whole way of life. Those who are nearest and dearest to the convert feel they have been stabbed in the back. The father of the convert is ashamed to walk down the street. The family may disown the new believer in an attempt to rebuild honour in the eyes of their community.

No wonder God often uses dreams to speak to Muslims. It seems he may have to dial them up directly to get their attention. It is reported that twenty five percent of Muslims who convert do so through dreams. And even then, like my friend Ahmet who once had a dream of Christ, this direct action may still not be enough. Ahmet is still sitting on the fence. But there is time yet. Like Okan we have not seen the last chapter in his life either.

When we extend the invitation to Muslims we must accept that the process will be long. It will often seem like one step forwards and two steps backwards. The cultural gap makes it very difficult to read what is going on. We will frequently be caught off guard by unanticipated actions and reactions.

For a couple of years Ali faithfully attended Sunday morning worship and Thursday evening Bible study. Then suddenly, without warning, he stopped coming. We heard that his mother was sick and he couldn't leave her. We heard that a relative was running for political office and he was keeping a low profile for his sake. But none of it really made sense to us. Six months later he gradually became part of the scene again. We never did discover the real reason for his absence.

Then there is the problem of grace itself. Of course, we all have problems with grace. Common human pride rebels. Earned salvation would be so much more satisfying, or so we think. But for people of an honour-shame culture, grace is particularly difficult. It is a shame to receive a gift without reciprocating. Gifts may be refused because they obligate the receiver to return the favour. But how can we get even with

God? Grace is the un-earned, un-merited, un-repayable gift. Where is the honour in that?

In honour-shame cultures, the burden of sin is felt more as shame than guilt. Paradoxically, the gift of grace may only serve to increase shame. How can we present the Christian Gospel in a way that connects? As we spend time with Muslims we will begin to see the world through their eyes. We will begin to know the Muslim heart. As we grow in our relationships with Muslims the Holy Spirit will give us ways and words that communicate the Gospel in a language that can be heard.

The shortest route to the Muslim heart is to follow the Jesus of the New Testament. Jesus fulfilled his ministry in an honour-shame culture, not a Western, guilt-oriented culture. We learn from Jesus that the Gospel needs to be incarnate, embodied. He did not announce the Good News in words only, he welcomed people personally, he embraced them, he included them in culturally powerful ways. He took their sin seriously, but it was not the first point of contact. When he did preach grace, he did so indirectly, he spoke in parables. It was not an in-your-face kind of grace. He gave people legroom. Jesus models the defense-melting power of *incarnate* grace.

All ministry is by faith. We may be aware of only a small part of what God is doing in a person's life. Much will happen that we simply will not understand. But by faith we jump in and trust the Lord to graciously use us. And he does use us. As we stand back we realize that over time there is change. We trust God to bring to a good conclusion the things he has begun—because that is the kind of God he is. And we remember this, that one day there will be people from every cultural background standing in worship before the Lamb.

Testimony vs. debate

When I say that it is easy to talk about Christianity with Muslims, I need to add that this discussion will likely be at the level of debate. And while it is good to understand some of the basic differences between Islam and Christianity and to be familiar with the arguments, I don't believe that many Muslims will come to a saving faith in the Lord Jesus through debate. Debate creates winners and losers. In an honour-shame culture this is not especially productive. Apologetics is more helpful after conversion than before.

But testimony is different. Testimony is un-debatable. We share our experience. This is how it is with us. We will share in words, but also by our lives—likely much more than we realize!

At one point during our time in Turkey I was living alone for two weeks while Betty was visiting our family in Vancouver. I found out later that our neighbours had watched me like hawks during that time. They assumed that as a Christian, while my wife was away, I would run around with other women. That's what Christians do isn't it? When they saw that I didn't behave that way their attitude changed. One day when I stopped in to see Okan another man was there. I listened as Okan explained to him who I was. He finished with this: "He's a Christian, but he's clean!" Thank you Lord.

It is difficult to know when to move into a more active kind of testimony. First our words need to be earned. And this takes time. But there are moments when we draw on our deposit of spiritual boldness and offer to pray or speak very directly about Christ. There are times when it seems right to give a Bible, or some Christian literature. This fits best, however, when we are building on authentic presence and when we have begun to establish a real relationship.

In all this we depend on the Spirit of God to be at work in us and in our friends. First Thessalonians 1:4-6 is helpful.

> *For we know, brothers loved by God, that he has chosen you, because our gospel came to you not only in word, but also in power and in the Holy Spirit and with full conviction. You know what kind of men we proved to be among you for your sake. And you became imitators of us and of the Lord, for you received the word in much affliction, with the joy of the Holy Spirit...*

Notice how the Spirit is active in both the speaker and the hearer. The Spirit was at work in Paul and his co-workers so that the Word went out with the power and authority of God behind it. The Spirit was also at work in those who heard, convicting them, then leading them into the full joy of the Lord. We are not apostles, yet we are bold enough to believe that we will at least taste this experience from time to time, becoming partners with the Spirit of God himself in the powerful ministry of the Word.

So we do use words, but they will more often be words of testimony than debate. We will not gain much ground trying to argue truth piece by piece. What is powerful is coming alongside with our whole lives, allowing people to see a whole new way of living, a new circle of reality, a new construct. This becomes even more powerful as we connect our friends with the living church, and they catch a glimpse of this new reality in 3D.

The power of corporate testimony
One church in Vancouver has a Muslim family attending regularly. They love being part of that community. Recently they were looking for a new home, but it had to be close to the church because they didn't want to get disconnected from their church family! The church simply loved them, embraced them, and gave them space. They trusted God to complete his work in them according to his schedule.

Community is important for Muslims. This is reportedly one of the reasons so many black Americans are attracted to Islam—it gives them a place to belong. When Muslims, and other group-oriented people, see the Christian faith as a *corporate* experience it is easier for them to cross over. They have not just left their village to live a solitary life in the wilderness. They have crossed over into a new village. A new family is waiting for them. Often we see that people from group-oriented cultures are first converted to the church, then later they are converted to the Lord of the church.

But don't underestimate the culture-shock for Muslims attending a church service. They wear shoes in the sanctuary! Men and women sit together! People walk around and call out to each other across the room! They sing like soccer fans! Bare-armed women lead the program! The Sacred Book is tossed on a seat like a newspaper! How could the Holy God of heaven and earth be pleased with this profane performance?!

We need to pray hard for those we invite to church. Yet, if they come, and if they can get beyond the disturbing outward form of our worship, they may begin to see God with new eyes. The apostle John put it this way (1 John 4:12):

No one has ever seen God;
[but] if we love one another,
    God abides in us and his love is perfected in us.

God is present in our corporate life in a way he cannot be present in our private lives. The church is a dangerous place to be for the unbeliever. Corporate faith is infectious.

Cost effectiveness
One (Christian) man asked me: "Is it cost-effective to work with Muslims?" As you can imagine I was irked at the question and had to bite my tongue twice before answering! It troubles me that the question is even voiced. But there is an upside. Such a question cements our conviction that every human being is of immeasurable value to our Heavenly Father. God loved Muslims so much he was willing to give his only Son to redeem them from death. How do you put a price on that? The Kingdom of God is a not-for-profit operation! ...More on this later.

Nevertheless we do want to be effective. And the larger the cultural gap we stretch across in extending the invitation the more difficult it is to be effective. Reaching out to Muslims calls for a lot of listening. It calls for a large investment of personal time. It calls for sincere respect. It calls for a willingness to build bridges. We know what we have to share. We have discovered a great banquet. But it takes time to learn how to formulate the invitation in ways that are attractive to the Muslim heart. Some forms of evangelism are as attractive to Muslims as an invitation to a pig roast! But we can do better, and by God's grace we will.

O Lord, teach me to love.

Is it not supposed to be a family characteristic?
I know I am adopted, but I can learn.

Teach me to love as you love O Lord,
so that on the day you appear I shall be like you.

O Lord, teach me to love.

If I care enough I will figure out
how to speak the words of life in ways that connect.

O Lord, teach me to love.

I pray in the name of the one who loved Muslims so much
that he gave up his life for them,
so that if any one of them believed in him
they would not perish
but would have eternal life,
Amen.

8. Meeting Points

It must have been thirty-five years ago. I was crossing from New Brunswick to PEI on the old ferry affectionately known as the Abby. The trip that normally took forty-five minutes took four hours as the ice breaker patiently backed up and drove forward through the frozen sea. But I got talking with a fellow traveler and the time slipped by nicely over cups of coffee and wide-ranging conversation. By the time the ferry crashed though the last of the rafted ice at Borden we were like old friends. Until, just before we headed down to our cars, he tried to get me interested in a line of products he was selling. I will never forget the feeling of being deeply wounded—like a knife in the stomach. That man had befriended me purely for profit. I was not a real person to him, I was a business opportunity.

It is a real turn-off to discover that the person befriending you is only trying to sell you something. It is a form of prostitution. Our friendships must be genuine if they are to be meaningful. If "friendship evangelism" means making friends with people just in order to present the Gospel, I don't want any part of it. Our friendships with Muslims must be authentic in their own right. Friendship that is a means to an end is no friendship at all. When Jesus said to the disciples, "You are my friends," it was not a ploy to fulfill a hidden agenda, he loved them for who they were.

But where does this leave us? We are talking about extending the invitation. We want others to share in the Gospel feast. Isn't this done most effectively through meaningful relationships?

The messy, earthly reality is that we will struggle with our motives. We cannot know our own hearts fully. But let's strive for authenticity and transparency. Let's be like Nathanael, in whom was no guile (John 1:47). We will not be manipulative. We will treat people with respect, as fellow pilgrims on this earth. Our friendship is genuine when it is mutual, when we enjoy each other's company. It may even catch us by surprise. When I first thought of going to live in a Muslim country I must admit I wasn't anticipating the friends we would make.

Surprised by friendship

For all the ups and downs in our relationship, Okan and I grew to enjoy each other's company. He seemed to greet me with genuine warmth. I could hear it in his voice as he introduced me to his friends. And I, in turn, enjoyed dropping by to see him, often with a handful of pistachios in my pocket, or a couple of fresh Canadian cookies, to share in exchange for the ever-present tea. He used to give me little booklets by an early 20th century Turkish Muslim author who was somewhat conciliatory towards Christianity. I gave him a Bible and some other literature. We joked that in a year's time he would have changed his name to John and I would have changed my name to Okan—we would have converted each other!

In meeting with Ahmet at the mosque I also got to know Abdi who looked after the tea room. I found out he was originally from far off Rize, east of Trabzon on the Black Sea coast. This is the tea-growing region of Turkey. No wonder he brewed the best tea in town—and only thirty Turkish cents a glass. I often dropped by when it wasn't a lesson day to sit with a dictionary and a newspaper and some fresh tea. Abdi would sit with me briefly between customers and we would talk a little, my broken Turkish stretched thin.

Abdi is just about my age and we have children the same age. Ahmet was the scholar and teacher, but Abdi became a friend. We enjoyed each other's company. He works long hours seven days a week, so he has little time for reading. When I left Istanbul I went to see him and received the usual warm kiss on both cheeks. We chatted over tea once more, then, as I left, I gave him a DVD of the life of Christ. I wasn't entirely comfortable doing that. Would he think my friendship was only a ruse? Looking back I think our friendship is deep enough that he will understand.

Mahmud was the realtor who helped us find that first apartment in Istanbul. He seemed genuinely helpful and went out of his way to see that we were happily settled. Later I made a point of looking him up to thank him. It took me quite a while to find his office again in the maze of streets. When he saw me he first looked troubled. "Is everything OK? Is there a problem?" I assured him we were very happy. Then we settled down to tea and a chat. Later he asked me again if everything was OK. Perhaps he thought I was ashamed to bring up the problem.

As I dropped by from time to time, I discovered I wasn't the only one who took advantage of the teapot sitting on the little propane tank in the corner of his simple storefront office. I also got to know Murat, a building contractor, who spent his summers in Antalya doing construction work for foreigners. On my last visit to Mahmut I discovered that Murat had married a Russian girl since I saw him last. This big, burly construction guy was becoming domesticated. Mahmut and I grinned at each other as Murat walked past led by a pocket-sized puppy on a leash.

The time came to say goodbye to Yakub. He wasn't happy to see me go. In his folksy, poetic way he cast himself into a future afternoon when he would look up from his little stand and see John once again walking down the street towards him. Then, returning to the present, he reached into his pocket and handed me something. "A little gift," he said, "nothing really." It was a string of beads—Muslim prayer beads. His name was written on them. They were special to him. Someone had once given them to him and now he was giving them to me. "So that you will not forget me, when you are back in Canada."

Of course we pray for our friends. We do look for opportunities to share what we have discovered. We wonder how we can get the Living Word into their hands. Even so there is something very precious about the friendship itself. In friendship we come close to the heart of our Trinitarian, relational God. The friendship itself pulls us heavenwards. Friendship sets up resonances with the intimate exchanges of the Father, Son and Holy Spirit. We were created for friendship. When we, God-imaged as we are, find friendship with each other, we are drawn into alignment with the eternal purposes of God. Friendship is redemptively subversive.

Thinking outside the box store

A Christian worker who has spent a long time in Turkey once told me that most missionaries do their best work in the first couple of years. He responded to my surprise by pointing out that when we first come we are very needy. Our helplessness throws us into contact with our neighbours as we try to figure out how to order drinking water and where to get a new belt for the washing machine. We meet people on the bus and on the street. We are always asking for directions. But all these connections and possibilities dry up as we gradually become independent and self-sufficient in this new world. We don't need people any more, especially once we have our own car.

Then, too, when we first arrive in a country we are trying to learn the language. We are looking for opportunities to speak. This is the only way to learn. We even maximize our meetings by not buying all our groceries in one place. We buy small amounts at four or five different stores. We make a point of getting to know the owners so that we can talk more and expand our vocabulary. Later on we don't have time for all that.

I mention this because we can do this back in Canada. It is well known that it is the new converts who are most likely to bring outsiders to church. We who have been believers for a while spend more and more of our time within the circle of believers. Not only that, but we are simply creatures of habit. We drive the same road to work everyday. We run through the same supermarket. We maximize the use of time, but we minimize the opportunities for meeting people.

What would happen if we tried to think like the new Christian worker out on the field? We could buy at least some food at the little corner store. We could venture into new areas of the neighbourhood and city, take a different bus. We could explore more coffee shops. We could commit at least some time to this kind of intentional connecting. We can't scatter the Word without scattering ourselves.

When I lived in Vancouver I always got my hair cut at the same place every month. Later, on a trip back to Vancouver, I dropped into a barbershop in an unfamiliar part of the city. I noticed that the man was of Middle-Eastern origin. As we talked I learned that he had come from Iran as a refugee eight years earlier. We talked about his children and his experience in Canada. He told me that he hoped to return someday to his home country. He was concerned about the negative effect of a secular society on his children. I was full of questions and he seemed happy to answer. If I had been living there I would have made a point of going back to get to know him better. It would be the most natural thing in the world to invite him in for some tea. Besides, it was a good haircut!

The world at our door

Over a quarter of a million immigrants arrive in Canada every year. They come from all over the world, these days especially from Asia. Many are Christians when they arrive. Every year more Christian immigrants arrive here than the entire Christian population of Turkey. In fact much of the growth of Vancouver area churches is the result of Christian immigrants joining the churches or establishing new congregations.

But many of these new Canadians are not Christians. And this is a wonderful time to extend the invitation. There is a window of opportunity when people first arrive. They have been uprooted, willingly or unwillingly, from their own familiar world. They are navigating a huge cultural adjustment. All of the little things we take for granted, they are just learning. It all takes a huge amount of effort. It is like re-experiencing childhood, especially if they are also learning a new language. And just as home-grown Canadians are most likely to convert during childhood and youth, immigrants also are more open to the Gospel as they experience this kind of second childhood.

In our church in Vancouver we offered English classes to new immigrants. We asked them why they kept coming back when there were so many other options for learning English. They said, "Here the teachers love us." One woman listed all the challenges of the past week: maneuvering through the bureaucracy of getting a car on the road, sorting out schooling for the children, dealing with a break-in at home…. She said (through a translator), "This class is like an oasis for me."

Why do people come to Canada? They come for their own education or the education of their children. They come to join their families already here. They come for economic opportunities. They may come through no choice of their own, like the wives who are relocated here by their husbands so their children can get a Canadian education. The husbands remain overseas earning money while their wives figure out how to make this new life work. Or they come as refugees, no alternative but to try to begin a new life in this strange country. Many, like my barber, are marking time, dreaming of the day when they can return.

If we don't overcome our fear of immigrants it will easily turn to hate. In Turkey we noticed it was the foreigners who spent the least time with Turks who were the most negative about the country. The best way to move beyond fear is to get to know people. This means reaching out, crossing the street, wandering into unfamiliar areas of the city, speaking to strangers. If we think it is hard for us to build bridges, imagine how hard it is for the new-comer who is already overwhelmed by all the cultural adjustments. It is simply unrealistic to expect them to knock on our door.

In meeting immigrants we don't have to always hold the position of power. We don't always need to be the helper. They get tired of being needy all the time. (A few years overseas helps us see this well.) In their own country they may have been highly competent professionals. Imagine what it feels like to be reduced to baby talk as you struggle to learn a new language: "Me want dis."

We can come as equals, or as learners. "Please tell me about your country. How do you greet guests in your home? Why is Islam important to you?" We can take the time to learn about their holy days and times of celebration. We can stretch a little further outside our comfort zone and learn to give a simple greeting in their language. This means so much. We can learn their symbols of hospitality and so help them feel more at home.

When we eat together, either in their home or ours, our relationship grows in leaps. We are no longer strangers. Meals break down boundaries. Eating together cements friendships. When we eat together we enter into a kind of covenant relationship. You are one of us. We belong to you. From now on I will watch out for you and you for me. The Turkish word for friend, *arkadaş*, means "the one at your back"—the one who looks out for you.

There are many opportunities to help. Unless we ourselves have experienced the challenge of trying to get a foothold in another culture we have no idea of how much there is to learn. Where do you mail a letter? How do you write the address? What do you need to open a bank account? How much do you give to beggars? How do you order a taxi? But as we offer help we also offer our new friends the dignity of allowing them to help us once in a while. Perhaps they will bring us a special dish of food. And we will enjoy it, even though it seems foreign to us. We will offer them the gift of a truly mutual relationship, which is the only basis of true friendship.

Our son has a painting business. Before we left for Turkey I worked for him for a couple of weeks. We found ourselves painting in a Muslim home. We enjoyed getting to know the family. They have two teenagers, a boy and a girl, both doing well in school and very active in sports. They always greeted us respectfully and made a point of coming to us to say good bye when they left the house. The father insisted on making us frequent cups of tea. Their culture of hospitality extended equally to house painters—it was a good lesson.

The woman of the house talked more openly about her faith than her husband. I had lots of questions about the life of their mosque and we had some good conversations. It was easy to talk about our faith also. One day we got talking about prayer. At one point she called over to her husband, "See, I told you, He [God] is always listening!" When we left we gave them a New Testament and they seemed to appreciate it.

May God give us a sense of urgency. If we wait too long the window of opportunity will pass. After a few years these new Canadians will be new no longer, they will have become re-embedded in this new world.

....

O Lord, let me not sell out on the possibility of friendship
because of my love of convenience and efficiency.

Let me not be like Esau who sold his blessing
for the convenience of fast food.

Let me be more adventurous, more expectant,
more alert to your match-making.

O Lord, forgive me for not delighting in friendship.

Let me not come to the end of summer
to find the harvest is past
and my friends are few.

I pray in the name of him who ventured into Tyre and Sidon,
and the region of the Decapolis,
for the sake of a few new friends,
Amen

9. Crosswalk Economy

As a pastor people ask me how things are going at the church. I never know quite how to reply. We can measure nickels and noses. How do we measure influence? How do we measure relationships? How do we measure movement along the pathway of faith? The church may be a hive of activity, but how much of this adds to God's glory? And if assessment is so difficult "in house," how much more difficult "out on the street." Are we making a difference out there? Are there any new faces at the table? Perhaps we are just shuffling seats—a kind of ecclesiastical mad hatter's tea party!

We long for ministry techniques that deliver. We search the shelves for how-to titles: *Four Keys to the Muslim Heart, Three Moves in Cultural Integration, Two-Stage Evangelism, Keeping the Main Thing the Main Thing...*(!) And it doesn't hurt to work on this. At the same time we need to ask whether our obsession with religious technology is a kind of idolatry. God invites us to be partners with *him*, co-workers in *his* ministry of grace in this world. But we are reluctant to relinquish control.

Perhaps the way to move beyond utilitarian ministry is to move beyond utilitarian worship. Why do we fast and pray? Why do we study the Scriptures? Why do we seek the Spirit? Is it to be more effective, or is it because we enjoy the companionship of our Lord. Do we know God as Friend? Do we know him as Father?

The delight of God

I have always been intrigued by the story of Jesus' baptism. There he is, the preparation over, time at last to begin his messianic ministry. If ever there is a moment to polish religious technology surely it has come. Jesus will only get one shot at this. So where is the divine advice? Instead we get these obstinately low-tech words from heaven:

> *You are my Son,*
> > *whom I love;*
> > > *with you I am well pleased (Luke 3:22).*

What a powerful affirmation. What a benediction (lit. "good word"). No one can choose the word for the moment like God the Father. And these are his words for such a moment as this. Not, "Here are some tips on effective preaching," or, "Now some advice on crowd control." But a deep affirmation of their relationship. "You are not my servant, you are my *son*. You are not anyone else's son, you are *my* son. I not only *love* you, I am *delighted* in you." With these warm and deeply nourishing words Jesus is released into ministry. It is enough.

There is a place for learning how-to. We can begin by watching Jesus at work. But there is something more foundational in ministry. Ministry is not built on technique but on relationship. True, we are not Christ, but we are invited into an intimate relationship with Him. We have been immersed into Him. Our lives have been hidden in Him. He is the first of many sons and daughters. So it is right to receive these words to our own hearts also. Through Him they come to us. God the Father says to each of us:

You are my daughter, you are my son,
I love you;
I am delighted in you.

Here is *our* starting point also. It is the place we return to again and again. It is enough. It is enough even when we take our part in the suffering of the cross.

The gift of suffering

For it has been granted to you that for the sake of Christ
you should not only believe in him
but also suffer for his sake (Philippians 1:29).

Along with these words of Paul we remember too Jesus' announcement that he has come not to bring peace, but division (Luke 12:51). But here is the great secret of the Christian life. God's delight in us carries us through all kinds of suffering.

New believers don't have it easy in a Muslim context. Muslim background believers may, at least for a while, be cut off from their families. They may lose their jobs. Women may have difficulty attending Sunday worship. In one church some of the women faithfully attended the daytime, mid-week Bible-teaching, studying hard and growing in their faith, but they had to remain at home with their husbands and family on Sunday.

Sometimes it is the husbands who are restricted. My teacher Mahmut told me he worried about what his unconverted wife might do to him while he was asleep at night.

Other believers suffer bone-deep loneliness. A young university student helped Betty with her Turkish over the summer. It was a great time of fellowship for both of them. That fall she headed back to school in city of half a million souls where she had no Christian fellowship at all. Our Heavenly Father's delight in us sustains us through these difficult times.

Some believers try to keep their conversion a secret. One single older woman kept her church attendance hidden from her family. She wore her headscarf until she arrived at the door of the church building. She loved the church and was very active. But as she left she put her headscarf on again. We sympathized with her in her fear, but we longed for her to know the love of God in a way that overcomes all fear.

This was clearly the experience of another woman who went down to the police station and had the religion box on her identity card changed from "Islam" to "Christianity." This was a brave move given that these identity cards are to be carried at all times and are needed for numerous transactions in daily life.

While we were in Turkey we saw dramatic examples of the power of the love of God in times of deep suffering. Early in 2007 the country was shocked by the killing of Armenian journalist Hrant Dink. At the funeral his wife, Rakel, quoted John 15:13, "Greater love has no one than this, that someone lays down his life for his friends." This love, she said, is found only in the Messiah. Speaking as though to her dead husband she said, "I owe it to Jesus that I was capable of penning this, my beloved." Half of Turkey watched the Christian ceremony on television and saw and heard her powerful testimony. What an extraordinary opportunity for Christian witness in a land where 99% are Muslim.

The promise of resurrection

The assurance of our Father's love is vital. But the promise of resurrection doesn't hurt either! When Jesus got the news about Lazarus being sick (in John 11) he said to his disciples, "Come on. Lets go. Our friend needs help." But the disciples were afraid to venture that close to Jerusalem where only recently Jesus had barely escaped with his life. A second time Jesus urged them to come with him. Finally, unexpectedly, it is Thomas who says, "Come on guys. We might as well go and die with him." He is not exactly a beacon of confidence, but at least he has the courage to speak up. And at least he has the courage to obey.

It is in this context that Jesus declares: "I am the resurrection and the life," and goes on to raise Lazarus. Is not this a powerful antidote to our fear—the promise of resurrection? Resurrection hope sets us free to obey no matter what may lie ahead. What a gift! What can the enemy do to us? When our fear of death is gone we are no longer afraid of crossing the street to speak to a stranger, or of crossing the ocean.

Perhaps it is natural to experience increased anxiety living in a strange land. But here in Canada we also live with fears. How do we overcome? True, the physical cost of discipleship for us in Canada is not high. Nevertheless suffering has a central place in Christian experience. We may not often use the language of suffering in the church in Canada, but the reality of suffering remains wherever ministry remains true. There is no ministry without suffering. We follow a crucified leader. And he invites us also to take up our cross and his cross.

There is the suffering of misunderstanding. There is the suffering of looking foolish and unsophisticated. There is the suffering of being uprooted, as we are called and sent out into the world. Then too there is the suffering of weakness and ineffectiveness.

Failing gracefully

The measurable output of Jesus' ministry is not impressive. A dozen disciples of dubious character. A ministry cut short. A shameful death. Nothing to impress a pulpit committee. So how do we assess the ministry of Christ? Did he make good use of his time? How do we account for it?

And what about our own ministry? There may be very little to see. "How many did you lead to the Lord?" we are asked. We change the subject. I went to Turkey to teach. I returned to Canada because getting to that level of language ability didn't seem attainable in my working lifetime. Were those three years wasted? What about the financial cost? How do we account for that investment of time and resources?

But when we bring these questions of effectiveness to the Gospels we are left with an awkward silence. The ministry of Christ is weighed in different scales. We don't find categories of efficiency. What we do find is that his relationship with his father is not broken. We find that through all the ambiguity of ministry, Jesus is at peace. He tackles each assignment with quiet confidence until we hear his closing assertion, "It is finished." Except for those few tortured hours on the cross, he knows who he is, he is the son of his father. It is enough.

We are called first to a relationship. Ministry is secondary. So we are cautious with assessment tools. At best they only capture a part of our Christian life. Sometimes they just miss the point. It may be that our days of seemingly great productivity at the storm center of ministry will be shown to be insubstantial on the day of the great refining fire. It may be that the small and hidden acts of service will remain as gold. There is also the strange paradox that God chooses to accomplish his purposes in weakness.

> *But God chose what is foolish in the world to shame the wise; God chose what is weak in the world to shame the strong; God chose what is low and despised in the world, even things that are not, to bring to nothing things that are, so that no human being might boast in the presence of God (1 Corinthians 1:27-29).*

But though we do not boast in ourselves, there is One who boasts in us. He carries our photo in his wallet. He delights in us. It is enough.

We need a kind of shyness around the economics of ministry. We have been adopted into the family of God. Surely the travel expenses are at least as much his responsibility as ours. Perhaps it is impolite to glance over as he writes the cheque.

The Engel scale

Having said this there are, in fact, ways to evaluate ministry that give us practical encouragement. Here are two models. The first is the Engel Scale of Evangelism so named for the author who publicized his thoughts on this in the 1970s.

Think of a scale running from minus ten to plus ten. All human beings fit on that scale somewhere. At minus ten are those who have no sense of a god of any kind. At minus nine are those who believe in some kind of fate or impersonal chance. As we move up the scale we come to people who have some idea of a personal god, then those who accept that this god reveals himself in written form. Eventually we come to those who have an understanding of the Messiah and the Gospel. Until, at the zero mark, we meet men and women who have crossed over, they have converted to the Christian faith, they believe and are saved. They go on to mature and grow in their faith, stage by stage, until, moving towards a plus ten, they are deeply discipled, and discipling believers.

What is helpful about this model is the idea of the spiritual life as a continuum. Of course we all want to be where the action is at point zero. But it is also as important to help people move from a minus ten to a minus seven. God will use many people to help the pilgrim on her way. He will do so because our gifts are all different. In a healthy congregation different people will be actively using their gifts at different points along the line.

Yes, it is true that everyone needs to be born again, but we don't all have to work in obstetrics. May we be content to make our contribution at the point where the Lord of the church has gifted us, even though that might not be where all the cheering is going on.

This model is also useful for helping us understand the challenges of ministry in the 21st century. There was a time, a generation ago, when a large percentage of Canadian society was familiar, not just with the idea of a personal god, but also with the claims of Christ and the Gospel. Many people were already at only a minus one or two on the Engel scale. The church could focus on the conversion point because the ground work had already been laid.

But those days are over. We may occasionally run into people who simply need to be encouraged to confess what they already know and believe, but they are getting fewer. Many more do not even know the basics of the Christian faith. They are back at a minus six or less. We are not talking about new immigrants at this point, but people who have grown up next door to us. They are biblically illiterate. They simply do not live out of a Christian world view. Like the serious young man I met in a coffee shop whose world view was shaped by the Star Wars movies and the teaching of the Jedi Council.

It is helpful to see that God is calling us to come alongside people where they are in their pilgrimage. There may be times when we have the privilege of standing with them in the baptism tank. More often we will be helping them at some other point of the journey, perhaps even helping them take their first steps along the pilgrim way. Clearly we will have to do much listening before we can speak intelligently into their lives. Otherwise we will discover that we are speaking a language that has no meaning for them. Plug 'n play evangelism techniques don't cut it in the 21st century.

The centered-set model

The second model is the centered-set model. Mathematicians talk about two kinds of sets. One is a bounded set, the other a centered set. The members of a bounded set are members by virtue of being inside the boundary. The members of the centered set are members by virtue of their relation to the center.

In the life of the church the centered set model is helpful in keeping us focused on Christ. Though we will not "arrive" in this life, we are living an authentic Christian life when we are moving towards him. Ministry is about encouraging others in their movement towards Christ.

This model takes the focus off the boundary crossing (the moment of conversion) and turns us towards Christ. We still believe there is a real crossing over point. But we accept that God knows more about that than we do. In fact we may know much less about when and where this happens than we think.

I remember a man from a Buddhist background who claimed that he wasn't a Christian. But he read his Bible every day and prayed to Jesus every day. Had he crossed over? For that matter just when and where did the twelve disciples cross over?

For people, like Muslims, coming out of backgrounds that are very different from ours, conversion may seem complex and drawn out. If we can keep our eyes on Christ at the center we will be less anxious about the details of the boundary crossing. Like the person who flies from Vancouver to Seattle we know there must have been a boundary crossing somewhere, but the exact timing is unclear, and when the day is over, not that important.

All of this is to say that if we insist on evaluating effectiveness by counting border-crossings we may be unnecessarily discouraged. If we ask whether we are effective at helping people, at whatever stage they are, move closer to Christ, we may be more encouraged. Certainly in our work with Muslims with their long process of conversion we are simply thankful that our Lord has allowed us to walk with them for part of their journey.

A divine snail's pace

We try to be attentive to the moment of conversion because we believe in heaven and hell. Our thinking is captured in the famous question, "If you die tonight, do you know for sure you will go to heaven?" And there is no doubt that for the person somewhere in the world who loses his life as I write this paragraph this a crucial concern. But the question may also produce unhelpful anxiety. It is, after all, a hypothetical question. Most of us will not die tonight. If we focus exclusively on the moment of conversion we both miss much and take on too much.

May we set each other free to be less driven to counting conversions. How good it is to simply be present with someone, in Jesus' name. We are confident in God's affirming smile on us as his children. At the same time we are authentically present with our friend, attentive to where he or she is in their spiritual journey. How powerfully God can work in that moment as he fulfills his own purposes according to his own schedule—always on time and on budget.

… … … … … … … … …

O Lord, I wish you would hurry up.
Do you not realize how late it is?

Could you not make more efficient use of my time?
(I promise not to take all of the credit.)

Sometimes you seem so foreign.
Your ways are not my ways.
Your values are not my values.

We need to talk more.
Clearly I still need some realignment.

I pray in the name of the One who wasted thirty years of
perfectly good earth time,
Amen.

In closing...

These meditations are written in the context of our actual experience of living among Muslim people. Often I have simply quoted from our newsletters. I am not writing ideologically, this is how it was with us. Getting to know our Muslim neighbours in Turkey was an immense privilege.

How precious it is for us to have Muslim friends who have become like family, who would take us into their homes at a moment's notice. When we say goodbye we all have tears in our eyes. With some of them we are able to keep in touch by email. For all of them we can pray that God will complete in them what he has begun.

So we circle back to the place where we began. Mission begins and ends with God. It is he who calls, and it is he who brings to completion. God is patient. This means that he delays judgment, for our sake. God is love. This means that he will go to any lengths to save one person. Certainly he will not hesitate to uproot us out of our predictable, manageable lives if he can use us to bring home one lost pilgrim. This is not about us, it is about *him*. We remember the emphasis of Acts 2:47, "And the *Lord* added to their number day by day those who were being saved."

When we extend the invitation we receive much more than we give. Not only are we blessed with new relationships, we are also blessed with new perspectives. Betty and I have lived where there are almost no churches. Because of this we see now how precious each church is. In the past we might have looked at a little, struggling congregation and wondered if it was time to close the doors. Now we think, if only we could have that group of fifteen believers, with all their depth and maturity, over in that Muslim country! There are no throw-away congregations. Each one offers a unique window on the Kingdom of God. Each reflects the heart of God differently. How God loves each church!

And then there is Easter. Living in a Muslim country has given us a deeper appreciation of Easter. Each year in Turkey, as in all Muslim countries, each family celebrates Korban Bayram, the Sacrifice Holiday, by offering a sheep, or, for those who can afford it, a bull. We watched as our neighbours killed, skinned and cut up their offerings to Allah, their back yards running red with blood. Afterwards they kindly shared with us from their rare bounty of meat. But how we longed to help them see the once-for-all cross of Christ.

How blessed we are to know Jesus, the Lamb of God, the final sacrifice. Easter is not about eggs or rabbits—*God forbid!* Easter is about Jesus, the one and only Son of the Father, hanging on the cross, the ground beneath running red.

Lets return again and again to the foot of the cross to bow in humility and awe, rejoicing in the love of God who has set us free once and for all from the bondage of sin, the deceit of the devil, and the fear of death.

Easter is a time of rehearsing, recalibrating and re-anchoring. We gather, as a community of believers, and remind ourselves of the bitter heart-ache and the leaping joy of the cross. This tough-as-nails love reveals the heart of God himself. It is all so personal.

Amazing love! how can it be
That Thou, my God, shouldst die for me!

We are called to extend the invitation. But it is to an unusual banquet. To those passing by there is not much on the table, but to those with eyes to see, the bread and the cup overflow with life. It is a meal that satisfies the deepest hunger. It is a meal that shouts: *Welcome home, beloved of the Lord!*

....

Come, everyone who is thirsty, come to the waters;
and he who has no money,
come, buy and eat!

Come, buy wine and milk
without money and without price.

Why do you spend your money
for that which is not bread,
and your labor for that which does not satisfy?

Listen diligently to me,
and eat what is good,
and delight yourselves in the richest of food.
Isaiah 55:1-2

Made in the USA
Charleston, SC
17 May 2010